£1~50

Who wants to be a
Edinburgher?

Jan-Andrew Henderson
& Barry Gordon

BLACK & WHITE PUBLISHING

First published 2004
by Black & White Publishing Ltd
99 Giles Street, Edinburgh EH6 6BZ

ISBN 1 84502 016 2

British Library Cataloguing in Publication Data:
A catalogue record for this book is available
from the British Library.

Cover design by McCusker Graphic Media

Printed and bound by AIT Nørhaven A/S

CONTENTS

INTRODUCTION   v

THE QUESTIONS

1   People   1
2   Places   13
3   Buildings   25
4   History   37
5   Sport and Leisure   49
6   Customs   61
7   Weird Edinburgh   73
8   The Arts   85
9   Leading and Lagging   97
10   Miscellaneous   109

THE ANSWERS   121

HOW DID YOU DO?   152

INTRODUCTION

It's hard to pick out a single characteristic shared by the people of Edinburgh. In fact it's hard to say what you even call them. Edinbrughians? Edinburghers? We've settled for Edinburghers. It may sound like fast food but it's easy to spell. That doesn't get us any closer to defining what actually *makes* an Edinburgher – especially since everyone living in the city seems to have come from somewhere else. Even the tour guides have foreign accents and I defy you to find a bar in Edinburgh that doesn't have an Australian behind the bar.

So what *does* make an Edinburgher? The answer is as incredibly complex as the city itself – so we'll make up our own definition. Edinburgh is just a village all dressed up as a major city and you're a real Edinburgher if you care what happens to the place.

Ah. But how deep is your love? Are you an Edinburgher or just a tourist who hasn't got round to leaving? Read on and see ...

'Here I stand at what is called the Cross of Edinburgh, and can in a few minutes, take fifty men of genius and learning by the hand.'

Mr Amyat, King's Chemist

Edinburgh is a small city with big names. From Sean Connery to Greyfriar's Bobby, from Robert Louis Stevenson to Alexander Graham Bell, Auld Reekie teems with those who touched hearts, captured the imagination and influenced the outside world. Visionaries, innovators, inventors, even criminal masterminds – we've got the lot.

When it comes to distinguished descendants, the city of Edinburgh has one of the largest families in the world. Nearly every street, building or park is named after someone famous or infamous in the town's lineage, so let's get started and see who you know.

1

1 What type of dog was Greyfriar's Bobby?

a	Jack Russell	b	Scottie
c	Skye terrier	d	Police sniffer dog

2 At which school did James Bond creator Ian Fleming study?

a	Fettes College	b	Edinburgh Academy
c	Boroughmuir	d	Heriots

3 Sean Connery used to be a nightclub bouncer and coffin polisher before becoming a famous actor. What other job did he have in the 1950s?

a	Postman	b	Milkman
c	Plumber	d	Bus driver

4 John Gibson is Edinburgh's longest serving – and oldest – newspaper columnist. Which paper does he write for?

a	*Scotsman*	b	*Scotland on Sunday*
c	*Edinburgh Evening News*	d	*Herald & Post*

5 Queen Street is named after which Queen?

a	Queen Charlotte	b	Mary Queen of Scots
c	Queen Elizabeth II	d	Queen Elizabeth the Queen Mother

6 Which great Edinburgh actor starred in the St Trinian's series as the school's headmistress and her brother?

a	Alistair Sim	**b**	Ewan MacGregor
c	Sean Connery	**d**	Alan Cumming

7 Which popular rock singer went to Broughton High School?

a	Eddie Reader	**b**	Shirley Manson
c	Annie Lennox	**d**	Lulu

8 What was Tony Blair's nickname at Fettes College?

a	Fleegle	**b**	Loopy
c	Millie	**d**	Dopey

9 James Gillespie, founder of Gillespie's Hospital, manufactured which product?

a	Tobacco	**b**	Firearms
c	Absinthe	**d**	Snuff

10 What do Giuseppe Garibaldi, Samuel Pepys, Benjamin Franklin, the Queen Mother, Yehudi Menuhin and Sean Connery all have in common?

a	They were (or are) Freemen of the City of Edinburgh	**b**	They had Edinburgh streets named after them
c	They all have timeshares at the Balmoral Hotel	**d**	They were all born in Edinburgh

11 John Knox was mistaken for what on his return to Edinburgh in 1558?

a	A tourist	b	An aristocrat
c	A king	d	An Englishman

12 Which famous architect designed the National Monument on Calton Hill?

a	William Henry Playfair	b	Robert Adam
c	William Hamilton Beattie	d	Alexander 'Greek' Thomson

13 George Boyd built a wooden bridge across the Nor' Loch so people could visit his shop. What kind of shop was it?

a	A tobacconist's	b	A butcher's
c	A chemist's	d	A tailor's

14 Charlotte Square was designed by Robert Adam. The statue inside the square is a memorial to whom?

a	Prince Albert	b	James VII
c	Robert Adam	d	An Unknown Soldier

15 Adam Smith, buried in Canongate Kirkyard, was the father of what?

a	Communism	b	Capitalism
c	Catholicism	d	Socialism

16 Who was Scottish Widows' most famous customer?

a	Sir Walter Scott	**b**	Sean Connery
c	Queen Victoria	**d**	Andrew Carnegie

17 What was sold by Harry Tranter with his famous sign ENGLISH SPOKEN, AMERICAN UNDERSTOOD?

a	Postcards	**b**	Haggis
c	Directions	**d**	The Scott Monument

18 What does it say on the tombstone of John Porteous?

a	Jhon Porteous	**b**	Killed by Indians
c	Murdered	**d**	Ayne true villean

19 According to legend, what was Deacon Brodie hiding in when he was arrested?

a	A coffin	**b**	A wardrobe
c	A brothel	**d**	A pantomime horse

20 How did 18th-century General John Reid combat the stress of military campaigns?

a	Taking long baths	**b**	Writing romantic short stories
c	Composing flute sonatas	**d**	Painting portraits of his soldiers

21 What connection does Sir Arthur Conan Doyle's monument in Picardy Place have with the building positioned directly behind him?

a	It's the setting of his first Sherlock Holmes story	**b**	His mother ran a boarding house there
c	It was his main Edinburgh residence	**d**	He died there

22 Inventor of the telephone, Alexander Graham Bell, was born in Charlotte Square. In which country did he die?

a	New Zealand	**b**	Wales
c	Canada	**d**	France

23 Maggie Dickson was hanged in the Grassmarket. On the way to her burial how was she brought back to life?

a	By the jolting of the cart carrying her	**b**	Mouth-to-mouth resuscitation
c	A witch's brew	**d**	Throwing a pail of water on her

24 Who was born in Portobello in 1870?

a	Sir Harry Lauder	**b**	Tom Mix
c	Stan Laurel	**d**	Joseph Locke

25 What did the famous geologist and author Hugh Miller do in Portobello that same year?

a	Drown	**b**	Discover tectonic plates
c	Shoot himself	**d**	Get arrested for nude bathing

26 Which journalist and presenter was born in Edinburgh in 1919?

a	Magnus Magnusson	b	Ludovic Kennedy
c	Alastair Cooke	d	Robert Kilroy-Silk

27 What famous poet honeymooned in Edinburgh in 1811?

a	Percy Shelley	b	Lord Byron
c	William Wordsworth	d	Keats

28 Who is the current Edinburgh Festival Fringe Director?

a	Robert DeMarco	b	Liam Rudden
c	Paul Gudgin	d	Andrew Eaton

29 In Blackfriars Street in 1506, Walter Chepman and Andrew Mylar produced Scotland's first what?

a	Printed book	b	Newspaper
c	Magazine	d	Arts festival

30 There is a statue of the Duke of Wellington on a horse outside Register House. What was his mount's name?

a	Copenhagen	b	Cardinal
c	Nosey	d	Metaxis

31 What did Dr Johnson throw out the window of the White Horse Inn?

| a | His trousers | b | James Boswell |
| c | His diary | d | His lemonade |

32 Why did Queen Victoria knight Sir John Steell?

| a | He made her laugh | b | She liked his sculpture of her husband |
| c | He punched the French Ambassador | d | He named all his children after her |

33 James Braidwood founded Britain's first what?

| a | Municipal Fire Department | b | Department store |
| c | Whisky distillery | d | Nudist colony |

34 What is notable about the Abraham Lincoln statue in Calton Cemetery?

| a | Lincoln is clean shaven | b | It was the first erected outside the USA |
| c | It commemorates Scots who fought for the South | d | It has the wrong birth dates on it |

35 The poet Robert Fergusson died in the Edinburgh Bedlam after which unfortunate incident?

| a | Drinking medicinal spirit. | b | A fight with another inmate |
| c | Falling downstairs drunk | d | Reading a particularly bad review |

36 How old was he?

a	19	**b**	21
c	24	**d**	28

37 Which style of verse, adopted by Robert Burns, did Fergusson make popular?

a	The Standard Habbie	**b**	The Edinburgh Couplet
c	The Colloquial Stanza	**d**	The Scots Quair

38 What was Jesse King better known as?

a	Big Jessie	**b**	The Morningside Ogre
c	The Clermiston Ripper	**d**	The Stockbridge Baby Farmer

39 Which Scots heroine went to boarding school in Old Stamp Office Close?

a	Elsie Inglis	**b**	Flora MacDonald
c	Mary Erskine	**d**	Jenny Geddes

40 What was Major Thomas Weir known as?

a	Tommy Atkins	**b**	The Wizard of the West Bow
c	Major Tom	**d**	Tam O' Shanter

41 What was John Graham of Claverhouse known as before he became Bonnie Dundee?

a	Roving Jo'	**b**	The Camperdown Hero
c	Dam'ned Graham	**d**	Bluidy Claver's

42 What was Robert Burns' sweetheart, Mrs McLehose, better known as?

a	Clarinda	**b**	Marigold
c	Henrietta	**d**	Clarissa

43 Who was removed from Edinburgh's coat of arms in 1562?

a	St Giles	**b**	St Andrew
c	St George	**d**	St David

44 Students of 19th-century professor and philosopher Dugald Stewart said there was 'eloquence in his very' what?

a	Spitting	**b**	Breaking wind
c	Sneezing	**d**	Coughing

45 Who is regarded as the greatest philospher to have written in the English language?

a	David Holmes	**b**	David Hogg
c	David Hume	**d**	David Locke

46 The oldest equestrian statue in Britain, erected outside St Giles' Cathedral (1685), is of King Charles II. What is he dressed as?

a	A Roman emperor	b	A soldier
c	A naval officer	d	A court jester

47 In 1650, the Marquis of Montrose was publicly hanged and then dismembered in Parliament Square. Where was his head fixed on a stake?

a	Above his grave	b	The entrance to Edinburgh Castle
c	On the Mercat Cross	d	Outside the executioner's home

48 Clerk Maxwell was greatly influential in the field of physics. For which discovery was he most highly regarded?

a	Microwaves	b	Nuclear fission
c	Solar power	d	Electricity

49 Famous for discovering logarithms, John Napier failed to graduate from which university?

a	University of Edinburgh	b	Heriot-Watt
c	Napier University	d	St Andrews University

50 The anaesthetic properties of chloroform help control pain. Who, on 4 November 1847, discovered it?

a	James Young Simpson	b	John Logie Baird
c	Alexander Graham Bell	d	Sir Thomas Falsaw

2

Places

At the Whitehall Theatre, Dundee, The Proclaimers singer, Charlie Reid, described the inspiration behind his band's popular ballad, 'Sunshine On Leith':

> I was on a flight back from America. I'd come out of a painful relationship and feeling depressed. Coming in to land, I looked out the window and saw dark clouds circling Edinburgh. Then, from out of nowhere, a ray of sunshine pierced the grey sky. It was shining on Leith. For the first time in weeks my heart lifted.

As Charlie Reid's story will attest, there are few places more inspiring in the world than Edinburgh. You could spend your whole life here and still never see all of its splendour. Just ask Robert Louis Stevenson who praised the city, saying, 'Every step is a revelation – an alleyway which reveals an ancient courtyard, or a wynd which opens up a new panorama.'

The city has a beach at one end, a world-famous bridge at the other and a large extinct volcano slap bang in the middle, and it's amazing just how easy it is to visit all three in an afternoon. In fact a half-hour walk in any direction and you might be in a palace, up a hill or even underneath the city.

Don't stray too far, though – you might end up in Glasgow.

1 In 2002 which popular festival venue was wiped out in a terrible fire?

a	Gilded Balloon	b	Assembly Rooms
c	Bedlam Theatre	d	Church Hill Theatre

2 What establishment is right above Gilmerton Cove?

a	A betting shop	b	A sauna
c	A children's nursery	d	A public toilet

3 Sean Connery was born and raised in which area of Edinburgh?

a	Niddrie	b	Muirhouse
c	Fountainbridge	d	Leith

4 The Black Watch memorial at the top of Playfair Steps commemorates which war?

a	The Boer War	b	WW1
c	Korean War	d	WW2

5 What is the name of Edinburgh's international airport?

a	Turnhouse	b	Idlewild
c	O'Hare	d	Holyrood

6 Where was the original location of the Scotsman newspaper's premises?

a	North Bridge	b	South Bridge
c	Rose Street	d	Lothian House

7 What was the name of the close where Robert Burns stayed, now incorporated into Lady Stair's Close?

a	Stanly Close	b	Mungo Close
c	Baxter's Close	d	Septy's Close

8 What is the nickname of Edinburgh's popular gay district?

a	Fountainpark	b	Wooftersville
c	Rainbow County	d	Pink Triangle

9 The Revolution nightclub on Lothian Road hosted a live televised show for which popular BBC TV music programme?

a	*Something Else*	b	*Old Grey Whistle Test*
c	*Top of the Pops*	d	*Later with Jools Holland*

10 What is Musselburgh's nickname?

a	The Shell	b	The Honest Toun
c	The Back O' Brunton	d	The Great Race

11 What gave Portobello its name?

a	The Duke of Beloque	b	A town in Panama
c	A local blacksmith's forge	d	A mushroom

12 What was Portobello once nicknamed?

a	Harry's Beach	b	The Scottish Brighton
c	The Black Bay	d	Handy Sandy

13 When was the port of Leith incorporated into Edinburgh?

a	1920	b	1925
c	1938	d	It's still officially separate

14 What was Newhaven's original name?

a	Cockleshell Bay	b	Our Lady's Port of Grace
c	Oldhaven	d	Clepsydra

15 Why is New Street so called?

a	It's named after William Newe	b	Fish from Newhaven was sold there
c	It connected the Old Town to the New Town	d	Because it was new

16 Where is the Scottish Storytelling Centre?

a	Leith Theatre	b	Netherbow Theatre
c	Above Jenny Haa's bar	d	Moray House

17 Deacon Brodie's last botched burglary was an attempt to rob what?

a	The Excise Office	b	The Bank of Scotland
c	William Buchanan's House	d	A hansom cab

18 What is carved into the pavements of Lady Stair's Close?

a	Quotes from Scottish writers	b	Lyrics of Auld Lang Syne
c	Sir Walter Scott's last words	d	George IV's address to Edinburgh

19 What will happen if the tree next to the Corstorphine Dovecot is cut down?

a	The owner's wife will die	b	A tree spirit will destroy the dovecot
c	The devil will steal the Lord Provost	d	The land will turn barren

20 What is the Edinburgh location that Shakespeare called 'Aemonie' in *Macbeth?*

a	Inchcolm Island	b	Arthur's Seat
c	Blackford Hill	d	Cramond

21 What runs all the way round Inverleith Park?

a	A bridle path	**b**	A bicycle lane
c	The Water of Leith	**d**	A barbed-wire fence

22 What is buried in Corstorphine Old Parish Church that shouldn't really be there?

a	A sheepdog	**b**	A witch
c	A Glaswegian	**d**	The Bishop of Lewis

23 Where was the infamous 'Hole in the Ground'?

a	Nicholson Street	**b**	Great King Street
c	The West Port	**d**	Castle Terrace

24 What were the first Wester Hailes community centres nicknamed?

a	The Barracks	**b**	The Sheds
c	The Huts	**d**	The Pits

25 Where did Edinburgh's gypsy colony once reside?

a	Marchmont	**b**	Stockbridge
c	Morningside	**d**	Little France

26 Where was the original Traverse Theatre?

a	The West Bow	b	St Stephen's Street
c	Great Junction Street	d	Priestfield Road

27 According to legend, where does the well in the Royal Botanical Gardens lead?

a	Hell	b	Australia
c	The Underground City	d	Edinburgh Castle

28 What is the road round Arthur's Seat known as?

a	Puffin Billy	b	The Invasion Highway
c	The Radical Road	d	The Breezy Bends

29 Where do cyclists encounter a strange optical illusion on Arthur's Seat?

a	The Innocent Tunnel	b	Duddingstone Loch
c	Passing Holyrood Palace	d	The Pollock Halls roundabout

30 Where did Scotland's royals reside before Edinburgh?

a	Dumbarton	b	Dundee
c	Dunfermline	d	Cowdenbeath

31 Whose headquarters are at 121 George Street?

a	The National Lifeboat Association	b	Alcoholics Anonymous
c	Historic Scotland	d	The Church of Scotland

32 What was inspired by an ornamental pond in Queen Street Gardens?

a	*Treasure Island*	b	*The Admirable Crichton*
c	*Robinson Crusoe*	d	*The Wreck of the Mary Deere*

33 Where did Sherlock Holmes investigate his first murder?

a	Lauriston Place	b	Picardy Place
c	Abbotsford Crescent	d	Cuddy Lane

34 What was first produced in Anchor Close in 1771?

a	The *Scotsman*	b	The *Reader's Digest*
c	The *Encyclopaedia Britannica*	d	The *Edinburgh Evening News*

35 In Fishmarket Close lived Edinburgh's last what?

a	Town Crier	b	Hangman
c	Lamplighter	d	Crimean veteran

36 Which famous poet lived in Carruber's Close?

a	Alan Ramsay	b	Robert Fergusson
c	Norman MacCaig	d	Violet Jacobs

37 Sir Walter Scott and Robert Burns only met once. Where?

a	The White Horse Inn	b	Findlay Avenue
c	Morrison Street	d	Sciennes House Place

38 Which ethnic landmark is across the street from their meeting place?

a	The Polish Embassy	b	A Jewish cemetery
c	The Institute for Native American Studies	d	The Ghurkha memorial

39 Where is the ruin of St Anthony's Chapel?

a	Arthur's Seat	b	Holyrood
c	Haddington	d	Dunbar

40 What was moved from Restalrig to Arthur's Seat?

a	St Margaret's Well	b	Sir Walter Scott's remains
c	A lead quarry	d	Edinburgh's only Pet Cemetery

41 What was **Princes Street** originally named, before George III lost his temper and demanded it be changed?

a	Castle View	b	St Giles Street
c	Princess Road	d	Glebe Street

42 Which place is famous for its links with the ancient Knights Templar order and tales of the Holy Grail?

a	Rosslyn Chapel, Roslin	b	Holyrood Palace
c	St Cuthbert's	d	Linlithgow Castle

43 Victims of the great plague in the 18th century were buried in which popular Edinburgh park?

a	Princes Street Gardens	b	Leith Links
c	The Meadows	d	Bruntfield Links

44 Where did **Greyfriar's Bobby** receive a bowl of food every day?

a	Greyfriars Kirk	b	Gray's Tea House on George IV Bridge
c	Grassmarket food stalls	d	Trail's Dining Room

45 Laurel and Hardy made their one-and-only appearance in Edinburgh at which cinema in 1939?

a	The Odeon	b	Green's Playhouse
c	Dominion	d	The Cameo

46 What is the name of Edinburgh's first new street since 1800?

a	Glasgow Street	b	Edinburgh Street
c	Fife View	d	The Walk

47 Which Stockbridge street was once described by English poet Sir John Betjeman as the most attractive street in Edinburgh?

a	Deanhaugh Street	b	Clarence Street
c	Ann Street	d	Dean Street

48 The ashes of College Wynd were rebuilt as which street?

a	Annandale Street	b	Guthrie Street
c	Leith Street	d	Nicholson Street

49 Which place finally opened to foot traffic in 1786?

a	North Bridge	b	South Bridge
c	George IV Bridge	d	Waterloo Place

50 Scotland's most famous duel, involving Court of Session judge Lord Shand in 1850, took place on a grassy slope below which famous Edinburgh landmark?

a	Arthur's Seat	b	Calton Hill
c	Blackford Hill	d	Salisbury Crags

3

Buildings

'The Castle looms – a fell, a fabulous ferlie. Dragonish, darksome, dourly grapplan the Rock wi claws o' stane.'

Alexander Scott,
Haar in Princes Street

From Victorian splendour to Georgian flamboyance, from medieval Old Town to New Town regality, Edinburgh's architecture is as monumental as that of any city across the globe.

William Playfair's majestic Royal Scottish Academy wouldn't look out of place in Athens or Rome. Ahead of its time, Robert Reid and Richard Crichton's towering Bank of Scotland head office could be best described as Italian 'Baroque 'n' Roll'. 'Edinburgh's Disgrace' on Calton Hill has become one of the tourist must-sees. Even the famous 'banana' and 'jigsaw' high-rise tenement flats in Leith and Dumbiedykes have a character and aesthetic all of their own.

However, Enric Miralle's costly Scottish Parliament – which has had more costume changes than a Madonna concert – may yet prove to be the new jewel in Edinburgh's architectural crown. Better still, Sir Terry Farrell, who designed the MI6 head office and Seoul International Airport, has been brought in as Edinburgh's new design tsar.

1 **What is the main tourist attraction at the Ocean Terminal Mall?**

a	The former Royal Yacht *Britannia*	b	The *QE2*
c	The marquee tent used for the 2003 Europe MTV awards	d	The life-size chessboard

2 **What is the nickname of the Leith high rise where the writer Irvine Welsh lived?**

a	The Banana Block	b	The Twin Towers
c	The Breeze Block	d	The Shoe Box

3 **Where would you find The Tower restaurant?**

a	Edinburgh Castle	b	Harvey Nichols
c	The Museum of Scotland	d	Ocean Terminal

4 **What is Jenners' claim to fame?**

a	It's the world's oldest independent department store	b	It was the first store to open on Princes Street
c	It's the Queen's favourite Edinburgh store	d	It has stocked all brands of perfume and aftershave ever made

5 **What is Sherlock Holmes's statue in Picardy Place frowning at?**

a	His pipe	b	A dog's footprint
c	Dr Watson	d	A taxi rank

6 The address 1 Princes Street belongs to which premises?

a	Caledonian Hotel	b	Balmoral Hotel
c	Burger King	d	Frasers

7 The cavernesque chambers of which pub inspired the idea for the 1995 hit movie *Shallow Grave*?

a	Bannermans	b	L'Attaché
c	Nicol Edwards	d	Whistlebinkies

8 What is the name of Hibernian football club's North Stand?

a	Famous Five Stand	b	The Hibee
c	Easter Hill	d	Frank Sauzee Stand

9 Which famous building on the south side sadly closed down in early 2004?

a	Queens Hall	b	Commonwealth Pool
c	Odeon Cinema	d	Pleasance Theatre

10 Why was Queen Victoria's statue moved from its original position outside Leith's Kirkgate centre?

a	A car crashed into it	b	She couldn't walk that far herself
c	To make way for a new monument	d	It was distracting traffic

11 In what type of building were the 2003 Europe MTV awards held?

a	A factory	b	A boat
c	A marquee tent	d	A hotel

12 Which popular music venue in Stockbridge's St Stephen Street was demolished before being rebuilt and turned into a restaurant?

a	Clouds	b	Cinderella's
c	Tiffany's	d	The Music Box

13 What resided in the middle of the London Road/Elm Row roundabout before the current clock?

a	An electronic road sign	b	Nothing
c	A statue of Sean Connery	d	An abstract steel monument

14 A full-scale model of which Edinburgh building is stored in New Zealand after the capital's Tattoo visited Wellington in the late 1990s?

a	Edinburgh Castle	b	Holyrood Palace
c	Edinburgh Zoo	d	Edinburgh International Conference Centre

15 What was the name of Scotland's first (and shortlived) cannabis café?

a	Fat Freddy's Cafe	b	The Purple Haze
c	Up in Smoke	d	The Humphrey Bogart

16 What was Edinburgh Castle's nickname in former times?

a	The Hot Rock	b	The Castle of Maidens
c	Auld Bumpy	d	The Grey Man

17 What was the famous Boundary Bar renamed in 2003?

a	The Middle Walk	b	The Dutch Elm
c	City Limits	d	The End

18 What is the Tron Church named after?

a	The Reverend Tom Tron	b	Charles I's spaniel
c	A weigh beam	d	A derivation of the word 'iron'

19 What was the name of Edinburgh's famous gay bar in the 1970s?

a	The Happy Hour	b	The Laughing Duck
c	The Bearded Imp	d	The Pink Panther

20 What was built out of 1,501,000 cartloads of earth from the foundations of Princes Street?

a	Lothian Road	b	The Mound
c	George IV Bridge	d	North Bridge

21 'The Wee Shop' based in Corstorphine is probably Scotland's smallest shop. How long is it?

a	Six feet	**b**	Four-and-a-half feet
c	Three metres	**d**	250 centimetres

22 Which phrase, constructed into gigantic letters, was strewn across a Dumbiedykes high-rise tenement?

a	This Way Up	**b**	Things Are Looking Up
c	Don't Look Down	**d**	To Let

23 The Scotmid supermarket situated at the foot of Leith Walk was converted from what?

a	A furniture warehouse	**b**	A church
c	Leith Central Station	**d**	A car showroom

24 Which of these *hasn't* been used as a venue for a Fringe production?

a	A jail	**b**	A telephone box
c	A car	**d**	A public toilet

25 The Forth Rail Bridge featured in scenes from which Alfred Hitchcock movie?

a	*39 Steps*	**b**	*The Birds*
c	*Psycho*	**d**	*Rear Window*

26 What oddities adorned the walls and roof of the Green Tree Pub (formerly the Brown Cow)?

a	Real foliage	b	Pictures of famous dictators
c	Painted-on cracks	d	Bullet holes

27 The castle esplanade was built in 1753 using rubble from what contemporary construction?

a	The Royal Exchange	b	Chessel's Court
c	The Mound	d	The New Town

28 What was the Dean Gallery Building previously used as?

a	A swimming bath	b	An orphanage
c	A workhouse	d	A glass blowing factory

29 The Festival Theatre in Nicholson Street was converted from what in the 1990s?

a	A bingo hall	b	A vehicle licensing office
c	A leisure centre	d	A sauna

30 Where was Edinburgh's highest ever tenement?

a	Haymarket	b	Parliament Square.
c	The Lawnmarket	d	The Grassmarket

31 What is reputed to be Edinburgh's oldest public house?

a	The White Hart	**b**	The Last Drop
c	Bannermans	**d**	The Beehive

32 What part of Edinburgh castle was built by French prisoners?

a	The cobbled walkway	**b**	The Half Moon Battery
c	The Dungeons	**d**	The main gate

33 What building is famously described as 'Edinburgh's Disgrace'?

a	The 12-columned acropolis on Calton Hill	**b**	The Scottish Parliament
c	The Scottish Executive Conference Centre	**d**	The Edinburgh International

34 The former GPO building on the east end of Princes Street is currently the capital's most high-profile what?

a	Advertising site	**b**	Property for sale
c	Festival venue	**d**	Property to let

35 What is unusual about St Andrews Catholic Church on Belford Road?

a	It's made of wood	**b**	It used to belong to the Church of Scotland
c	It was formerly a pub	**d**	It's shrinking

36 **Which pub had its walls and roof covered in bizarre curiosities?**

| a | The Canny Man | b | The Black Bull |
| c | The Queen Street Oyster Bar | d | The Auld Hundred |

37 **Who designed the National War Memorial Building?**

| a | Robert Adams | b | James Playfair |
| c | James Craig | d | Sir Robert Lorrimer |

38 **What is the Scott Monument's nickname?**

| a | The Pointy Bird | b | Scott's Ladder |
| c | The Gothic Rocket | d | The Big Quill |

39 **Who founded the Advocate's Library?**

| a | Sir George Mackenzie | b | James Rutherford |
| c | Charles II | d | John Knox |

40 **Clermiston Tower was built to celebrate which famous Scot?**

| a | Sir Walter Scott | b | William Wallace |
| c | Robert the Bruce | d | Robert Burns |

41 Who built Holyrood Palace?

a	Alexander Mission	b	Robert Mylne
c	Thomas Mann	d	Andrew Kay

42 Which building features Scotland's finest examples of pre-Reformation stained glass?

a	St Margaret's Chapel	b	St Mary's Church
c	Greyfriars Highland and Tolbooth Church	d	The Magdalene Chapel

43 The design of Stewart's Melville College was originally intended for what building?

a	The Houses of Parliament	b	Holyrood Palace
c	Fettes College	d	Westminster Abbey

44 What was odd about the service flats built in Orchard Brae between the World Wars?

a	They didn't have kitchens	b	They didn't have toilets
c	They had no front doors	d	They didn't have any letterboxes

45 Where are the last timber galleries in Edinburgh?

a	The Theatre Royal	b	Gladstone's Land
c	John Knox House	d	Torphichen Church

46 Edinburgh's first defensive wall was erected after what?

a	The battle of Flodden	**b**	The battle of Sark
c	The battle of Dunnechin Hill	**d**	The Holyrood Riots

47 What first opened in Ship Close in 1727?

a	The Royal Bank of Scotland	**b**	Edinburgh's first brothel
c	The Theatre Royal	**d**	Edinburgh's first swimming pool

48 What was discovered under 25 feet of rock and soil during the construction of the Union Canal in Kirkliston?

a	The remains of Robert the Bruce	**b**	The tusk of a mammoth
c	A poem written by Robert Burns	**d**	A tunnel full of gold

49 English prisoners had to leap a 12-foot gap between Borthwick Castle's towers if they wanted to be released. But they had to jump with which handicap?

a	Blindfolded	**b**	With hands tied behind the back
c	Backwards	**d**	Drunk

50 The Frasers building on Princes Street was once known as Maules. What other name did it go by?

a	Hepworths	**b**	Binns
c	Woolworths	**d**	Ferriers

4

History

'Edinburgh has been happily compared with a flag – a thing of history, worn and stained with old deeds and great days, and starred with burning names.'

Alanson B. Houghton

Edinburgh reeks of history. Here, you can drink in a pub haunted by Robert Burns, sit in a park used for burying plague victims and stand on the same spot as the last man to be publicly hanged in Scotland.

In 79 A.D., Agricola – the Roman Governor of Britain – was accosted at the River Esk (today Inveresk) by a Celtic tribe. This tribe, the Votadini, ruled the Forth River valley and were based at Dunedin – or Edinburgh Castle as it's more popularly known today. Since then, Auld Reekie has drowned more witches than you could shake a broomstick at, survived the ravages of the plague and harboured many of the world's most sinister criminals.

Edinburgh has been around for almost 2000 years but, like good wine, she ripens with age. Read on to find out about the city's links with Zeppelin bombers, tidal waves and Bonnie Prince Charlie.

1 In which year did Edinburgh become the capital of Scotland?

a	1066	b	1690
c	1633	d	1799

2 What was the name given to the plague of 1644?

a	The Black Death	b	The Black Plague
c	The Black Flu	d	The Black Cold

3 How many times in its past has Edinburgh actually been attacked?

a	17	b	35
c	Twice	d	Not often enough

4 Trams will soon reappear on Edinburgh's streets. In which year did they stop running?

a	1957	b	1962
c	1955	d	1949

5 What was the service number of the last tram?

a	42	b	99
c	101	d	172

6 Which of the following cities is Edinburgh not twinned with?

a	Vancouver	b	Florence
c	San Diego	d	Oslo

7 A mini tidal wave occurred in Leith as a result of offshore seismic activity. In which year did it happen?

a	2003	b	1973
c	1743	d	1843

8 One of Edinburgh's most spectacular riots occurred following the banning of which popular pageant?

a	Robin Hood	b	Peter Pan
c	Little Red Riding Hood	d	Dick Turpin

9 What percentage of Edinburghers died during the plague?

a	50%	b	20%
c	30%	d	75%

10 In which year did the great fire of Edinburgh wipe out most of the High Street?

a	1701	b	1899
c	1824	d	1556

11 Which wall was built around the city centre to help defend Edinburgh in 1513?

a	Dunedin Wall	b	Flodden Wall
c	Big Brick Wall	d	Great Wall of Edinburgh

12 In 1924 Edinburgh's first what began operating?

a	Telecommunications system	b	Public transport system
c	Radio station	d	Television station

13 What resulted in the cancellation of an historic theatrical occasion called by George V at the Empire Theatre in 1911?

a	A major fire	b	Balcony seats collapsed
c	Burst pipes flooded the theatre	d	George V sprained his ankle walking up the theatre steps

14 What length of time did Bonnie Prince Charlie spend in Edinburgh during 1745?

a	Nine months	b	14 days
c	Six weeks	d	The entire year

15 Burke and Hare were immigrants from which country?

a	France	b	Norway
c	Ireland	d	America

16 What did the *Great Michael*, pride of Scotland's navy, end up as?

a	A French prison ship	**b**	A Spanish slave ship
c	An Irish coal carrier	**d**	It sank off Scapa Flow

17 *Queen Margaret, Mary Queen of Scots, Robert The Bruce* and *Sir William Wallace* were the names of the last four what?

a	North British Corporation Railway Trains	**b**	Ferry boats to Fife prior to the construction of the Forth Road Bridge
c	Edinburgh trams	**d**	Coal Barges operating on the Clyde

18 What was the first vehicle pulled across the North Bridge when it opened?

a	A beer cart	**b**	A hearse
c	A cannon	**d**	A prison carriage

19 What did George IV wear under his kilt at an Assembly Rooms ball?

a	Nothing	**b**	Pink tights
c	A brace of pistols	**d**	Monogrammed underwear

20 Who granted Edinburgh its first extant Royal Charter?

a	Macbeth	**b**	Lulach the Simple
c	John Balliol	**d**	Robert the Bruce

21 The many blocked-up windows in Edinburgh were an attempt to get round what?

a	Window tax	b	Nosey neighbours
c	Deadly viruses	d	Sunlight tax

22 In 1574 in Fountain Close, Thomas Bassendyne produced Scotland's first printed what?

a	Bible	b	Map
c	Agricultural account	d	Tourist guide

23 Under which act was Maggie Dixon tried and sentenced to hang?

a	The Concealment of Pregnancy Act	b	Suspicion of Witchcraft Act
c	The Withholding of Information Act	d	The Concealment of Marriage Act

24 Which British king was born in Edinburgh Castle?

a	James VI	b	Charles I
c	Bonnie Prince Charlie	d	James V

25 When did the city's bus lanes first appear?

a	1974	b	1984
c	1948	d	1971

26 And on which street were they first visible?

a	Earl Gray Street	b	South Clerk Street
c	Princes Street	d	South Queensferry Street

27 What message was displayed on the floral clock in Princes Street Gardens to mark the end of WW2?

a	Our Finest Hour	b	Triumph Over Evil
c	Victory Is Ours	d	Our Greatest Achievement

28 Why did Edinburgh University temporarily move to Linlithgow in 1645?

a	The plague had broken out	b	The university burnt down
c	Student protests	d	Rents were cheaper

29 What did the Romans call the Celtic tribe who first inhabited Edinburgh?

a	The Votadini	b	The Emerald Azzuri
c	The Trinovantes	d	The Breuci

30 What was plotted at the Sheep's Heid Inn in Duddingstone?

a	The battle of Trafalgar	b	The battle of Prestonpans
c	The signing of the National Covenant	d	The Union of the Scottish and English Parliaments

31 What were caddies?

a	Street messengers	b	Horse-carriage drivers
c	Shoeshine boys	d	Street cleaners

32 Which club, founded by William Smellie, had Robert Burns as a member?

a	The Crochallan Fencibles	b	Royal Scots Club
c	Royal Archers Club	d	Edinburgh Poets Society

33 A disease referred to as 'The New Acquaintance' in 16th-century Edinburgh is known as what today?

a	Measles	b	Influenza
c	Chickenpox	d	Cancer

34 The best-attended lecture in the history of Edinburgh's medical school came in 1829. The body of which person had been supplied to the school for dissection?

a	Sir Arthur Conan Doyle	b	Deacon Brodie
c	Sir Walter Scott	d	William Burke

35 In which year did Princes Street's station, situated at the junction of Lothian Road and Rutland Street, close?

a	1960	b	1975
c	1980	d	1965

36 Fourteen bombing raids were experienced in Edinburgh during WW2. How many died in the raids?

a	237	b	17
c	None	d	99

37 Following the 1707 Act of Union with England, what did some locals dub Edinburgh?

a	A widowed metropolis	b	An angel with no wings
c	A lonely spinster	d	The capital of nothing

38 What did Lord Drumlanrig's son do while his father was witnessing the signing of the union?

a	Eat a boy servant he'd roasted on a spit	b	Murder his female servant with a walking cane
c	Shoot himself with a pistol	d	Eat his own hands

39 The first Edinburgh history book was published in which year?

a	1580	b	1899
c	1920	d	1792

40 Where in Edinburgh did King Malcolm III build his hunting lodge?

a	The zoo	b	Cowgate
c	Castle Rock	d	The foot of Arthur's Seat

41 Cloth sellers, beggars and fishwives' stalls on the High Street in the 15th century were known as what?

a	Luckenbooths	**b**	Portacabins
c	Brigstalls	**d**	Tradeboxes

42 Charles I's attempt to enforce his revision of the English Book of Common Prayer led to a riot in St Giles' Cathedral. What did cabbage seller Jenny Geddes throw at the minister to set it off?

a	A stool	**b**	A cabbage
c	A dagger	**d**	A bible

43 In 1328, the Treaty of Edinburgh ended which war that had taken place with England (in Scotland's favour)?

a	Wars of Dictatorship	**b**	Wars of Independence
c	Wars of Freedom	**d**	Wars of Hate

44 George Bryce was the last man to be publicly hanged in 1864. How many people turned up to witness it?

a	100,000	**b**	250,000
c	20,000	**d**	500

45 Name the processional ceremony that crowds stopped to watch during the opening of the old Scottish Parliament.

a	The Mode	**b**	The Riding
c	The Formality	**d**	The Ritual

46 Edinburgh's first-ever traffic signal began operating on 21 March 1928, at which junction?

a	Princes Street/Lothian Road	**b**	York Place/Broughton Street
c	Princes Street/Leith Street	**d**	Gorgie Road/Dalry Road

47 Where can you still find an old strip of tramline lying in the middle of the road?

a	Constitution Street	**b**	Queen Street
c	Waterloo Place	**d**	Tollcross

48 From what did citizens of Edinburgh and Leith come under attack on 2 April 1916?

a	The English Army	**b**	Earthquakes
c	Zeppelin bombers	**d**	Giant hailstones

49 What was the former Waverley Market in Princes Street used for during WW1?

a	The manufacture of tank parts	**b**	Sheltering from bombing raids
c	Secret council meetings	**d**	Weapon storage

50 What happened to prisoners when the old prison in the High Street was demolished in 1817?

a	They were pardoned	**b**	They escaped
c	They moved to Calton Jail	**d**	They helped in the demolition

5

Sport and Leisure

American tourist: Where's this Castle of yours?
Edinburgher: Behind you
American tourist: And the Scotch Monument?
Edinburgher: In front of you
American tourist: And where's Edinburgh's disgrace?
Edinburgher: They're playing away the day.

In the wild west (Glasgow), football *is* sport. And Edinburgh is home to two Scottish Premier League teams, Hibernian and Heart of Midlothian, both of which have loyal supporters. But here in the far east, the 'national game' competes with rugby for popularity. Meadowbank Stadium has been the venue for two Commonwealth Games. A new multimillion-pound sports arena in Sighthill looks to be on the cards and for those who can remember the days of Murrayfield Racers, the newly christened 'Carlsberg Capitals' are putting ice hockey back on the map in Edinburgh.

So, whether it's kicking, running or punching – and we're not talking about Jenners' January sale – Edinburgh takes care of your every sporting need, from judo to ju-jitsu, from speedway to speed skating – even tiddlywinks has its own club!

1 What was first played at Edinburgh's Leith Links?

a	Golf	b	Rugby
c	Football	d	Shinty

2 The Leith Victoria AAC is Scotland's oldest what?

a	Boxing club	b	Athletics club
c	Swimming club	d	Tiddlywinks club

3 Who are the sponsors on Hibs' jerseys?

a	Strongbow	b	Carlsberg
c	Lothian Regional Transport	d	Duff Beer

4 What is the former name of Edinburgh's ice-hockey team?

a	The Stockbridge Strikers	b	The Murrayfield Racers
c	The Meadowbank Arrows	d	The Edinburgh Rockets

5 What was Livingston FC's former name?

a	Meadowbank Thistle	b	Edinburgh Thistle
c	Currie Vale FC	d	Edina Hibs

6 Where was the first ever International Rugby game played in 1871?

a	Raeburn Place	b	The Meadows
c	Holyrood Park	d	Leith Walk

7 Martin Bell is associated with which rather unexpected sport for an Edinburgher?

a	Drag racing	b	Hot air ballooning
c	Alpine skiing	d	Pony trapping

8 Can you name the ex-Manchester United and Scotland footballer born and raised in Muirhouse?

a	Jim Leighton	b	Gordon Strachan
c	Brian McClair	d	Dennis Law

9 When was the last time Hibs won the Scottish Cup?

a	1888	b	1902
c	1956	d	1996

10 Who tried to amalgamate both Hearts and Hibs as one united team during the 1980s?

a	Wallace Mercer	b	David Murray
c	Sean Connery	d	Chris Robinson

11 Name Hibernian's campaign to stop it from happening?

a	Hands Off Hibs	b	Hibees Holdout
c	Leave Hibs Alone	d	Save Our Hibbies

12 Allan Wells won the 100 metres gold in the 1980 Moscow Olympics in how many seconds?

a	9	b	10.25
c	11	d	12.2

13 Gavin Hastings' record of 44 points scored in one test match lasted how long?

a	32 minutes	b	One week
c	Three months	d	It's still unbroken

14 What was World Lightweight Champion Ken Buchanan's trademark?

a	Paisley patterned gloves	b	Tartan shorts
c	A St Andrew's cross earring	d	He always won in the second round

15 Channel swimmer Ned Barnie used to shock people at Portobello Pool by high diving into what?

a	The most crowded part	b	The shallow end
c	A large bucket	d	A film of burning kerosene

16 How many caps did Andy Irvine win in his ten-year career playing rugby for Scotland?

a	48	b	51
c	63	d	72

17 What was champion golfer Tommy Armour's nickname?

a	Tartan Armour	b	Tom the Bonnet
c	The Silver Scot	d	The Iron Duke

18 Swimmer David Wilkie broke how many world, European and Commonwealth records in total?

a	10	b	20
c	30	d	None

19 What trophy did SPL team Livingston win in season 2003/4?

a	Brewers Cup	b	League Cup
c	Scottish Cup	d	B&Q Challenge Trophy

20 Chris Hoy won a gold medal in the 2002 Commonwealth Games for which sport?

a	Boxing	b	Cycling
c	Diving	d	Gymnastics

21 In 2000 which Scottish National race did the swimmer Danielle Barclay win?

a	200 metres breaststroke	**b**	100 metres freestyle
c	200 metres back-stroke	**d**	50 metres front crawl

22 Who are Hibs' Gordon Smith, Bobby Johnstone, Lawrie Reilly, Eddie Turnbull and Willie Ormand better known as?

a	The Fantastic Five	**b**	The Famous Five
c	The Fabulous Five	**d**	The Familiar Five

23 What is the name of the Scottish American Football team who play their home games at Murrayfield Stadium?

a	The Saltires	**b**	The Scottish Stags
c	The Caledonian Thistles	**d**	The Scottish Claymores

24 In 1938 the Hearts board proposed a move to a 'greenfield' site in which part of town?

a	Portobello	**b**	Straiton
c	Balerno	**d**	Sighthill

25 With which sport was former Hibs and Scotland goalkeeper Andy Goram also a Scottish internationalist?

a	Darts	**b**	Cricket
c	Tennis	**d**	Squash

26 For what was Hibernian's Easter Road ground pitch famous?

a	It's built on top of a graveyard	b	Its slope
c	It's the smallest pitch in Europe	d	It was blessed by the Pope

27 In which year were the first Commonwealth Games held in Edinburgh?

a	1964	b	1966
c	1968	d	1970

28 And the second?

a	1978	b	1980
c	1984	d	1986

29 At this event, Liz McColgan won gold in which race?

a	10,000 metres	b	Nothing, she came second in 4 races
c	The high jump	d	200 metres

30 What did John Mutai win in June 2004?

a	The Edinburgh Marathon	b	The Great Scottish Walk
c	The British Lightweight Boxing Championship	d	The Scottish Cup for Hibs

31 Stephane Adam scored in Hearts' Scottish Cup winning side of 1998. What nationality is he?

a	Belgian	b	Dutch
c	Swiss	d	French

32 Which team pipped Hearts to win the Scottish Premier League on the last game of the season in 1986?

a	Rangers	b	Aberdeen
c	Celtic	d	Dundee United

33 Hearts' new footballing academy was set up in 2004. Where is it based?

a	Tynecastle	b	Riccarton
c	Newcraighall	d	Musselburgh

34 What is the name of the Edinburgh Speedway team?

a	The Monarchs	b	The Kickstarters
c	The Trailblazers	d	The Speedkings

35 What is the name of Edinburgh's Celtic League rugby team?

a	Gunners	b	Cannons
c	Rockets	d	Devils

36 The women of ENC Onyx won the City of Edinburgh league for which sport?

a	Cricket	**b**	Hockey
c	Netball	**d**	Swimming

37 Which Hearts player scored a hat-trick against Rangers at Ibrox in 1996?

a	John Robertson	**b**	Neil McCann
c	Stephane Adam	**d**	Allan Johnston

38 What was the record attendance between Hibs and Hearts at Easter Road?

a	100,000	**b**	60,000
c	54,000	**d**	51,500

39 Where did Hearts football club take their name from?

a	Being in the middle of Midlothian county	**b**	The Heart of Midlothian stone mosaic on the Royal Mile
c	A dance hall called the Heart of Midlothian	**d**	A folk song

40 Where in Edinburgh is greyhound racing held?

a	Powderhall	**b**	Musselburgh
c	Dalkeith	**d**	Joppa

41 Which team did the Scotland rugby team play at its inauguration on 21 March 1925?

a	Ireland	b	Wales
c	England	d	France

42 What was the name of the vehicle Richard Noble drove when he broke the world land speed record in 1983?

a	Thunderbird 1	b	Thrust 2
c	Wheech 6	d	Mac 7

43 What speed did his car reach?

a	497 mph	b	556 mph
c	638 mph	d	712 mph

44 David Wilkie claimed gold at the Montreal Olympics in 1976. What 200-metre race did he win?

a	Front crawl	b	Breaststroke
c	Back-stroke	d	Butterfly

45 What did Lachie Stewart say to the legendary Ron Clarke after beating him in the 10,000 metres at the 1970 Commonwealth Games?

a	Sorry	b	Same time next year
c	Did I win?	d	It's unprintable

46 Traditionally, archers competed in Edinburgh for which trophy?

a	The silver arrow	**b**	The golden arrow
c	The bronze arrow	**d**	The silver bow

47 Which sport, in 1701, was banned from the streets of Edinburgh because huge crowds brought traffic to a standstill?

a	Boxing	**b**	Cockfighting
c	Tossing the caber	**d**	Archery

48 Formed in 1838, the Edinburgh club for which sport is also the 'Mother Club' for this sport throughout the world?

a	Long-distance running	**b**	Bowls
c	Curling	**d**	Shooting

49 James II once banned golf at Leith Links because it interfered with which other sport?

a	Archery	**b**	Highland Games
c	Clay pigeon shooting	**d**	Athletics

50 How did the great Edinburgh runner Eric Liddle die?

a	In a Japanese prison camp	**b**	A heart attack running the London Marathon
c	Of Cholera	**d**	He was hit by a tram

6

Homesick – an exile from Edinburgh bursting a paper bag at one o'clock

Anon

An elderly lady from Gorgie walks into a New Town grocer's and asks for a pint of milk. 'This stuff used to taste better when the dummie was still on the go,' she says to the shop assistant. 'I can't find my favourite gundie in any of the shops either.' The assistant looks confused. 'Not to worry, son, at my age I should be saving my money for the bell penny, anyhow.'

Today, you'll find more than just a New Town grocer baffled by the terms 'dummie', 'gundie' and 'bell penny'. Modern Edinburgh conventions usually consist of afternoon tea in Jenners, Hogmanay at the Tron, and spitting on the Heart of Midlothian. Washing your face in the morning dew following the Beltane Festival is another one of Edinburgh's contemporary customs. And imagine the festive period without Waverley's Winter Wonderland.

And while some customs may be long gone – as this next section proves – they're certainly not forgotten.

1 What language do the words 'Barry' and 'Raj' derive from?

a	Punjabi	b	Romany
c	Afrikaans	d	Weegie

2 The Edinburgh slang word 'barry' is to say something is what?

a	Good	b	Bad
c	Painful	d	Clever

3 Which day is reserved for late-night shopping in Edinburgh?

a	Sunday	b	Wednesday
c	Thursday	d	Saturday

4 What are Hearts fans affectionately known as?

a	The Jambos	b	The Heartbreakers
c	The Heart-throbs	d	The Jam busters

5 Coburg Street was originally a tolerance zone for what?

a	Prostitution	b	Cannabis smoking
c	Public drinking	d	Nude sunbathing

6 Whose statue stands across the road from His Majesty's Theatre?

a	5 minutes	**b**	10 minutes
c	Quarter-of-an-hour	**d**	2 minutes

7 Poet William Dunbar called Edinburgh 'a city of two contrasting faces: one rich, one poor'. These days people usually refer to Edinburgh as Pride and what?

a	Poverty	**b**	Prejudice
c	Prudence	**d**	Penance

8 What was carved above Willie Whitelaw's chair in St Giles' Thistle Chapel?

a	A big bee	**b**	A Great Dane
c	A large wren	**d**	A blue tit

9 Which of Edinburgh's many drinking clubs met in Fleshmarket Close?

a	The Thistle Club	**b**	The Marrowbone Club
c	The Monks of St Giles	**d**	The Borrowers

10 Why is Edinburgh's main waterway called the Water of Leith, not the River of Leith?

a	There's already a River of Leith in East Lothian	**b**	It's too small to be a river
c	It didn't sound right	**d**	Councillors wouldn't allow it

11 At Saughton Prison, 8am was the set time for what?

| a | Five minutes outside | b | Cell searching |
| c | Executions | d | Parole hearings |

12 Which street is said to have been built in a single day?

| a | Princes Street | b | Lothian Road |
| c | Leith Walk | d | Queen Street |

13 What is Edinburgh's popular festive attraction in Princes Street called?

| a | Winter Wonderland | b | Xmas Surprise |
| c | Snow Fun | d | Waverley Grotto |

14 Edinburgh's nickname Auld Reekie was first coined by folk from where?

| a | Glasgow | b | Leith |
| c | The Highlands | d | Fife |

15 Which meal of the day did the smoke bellowing above Edinburgh signal to them?

| a | Breakfast | b | Lunch |
| c | Dinner | d | Supper |

16 In the 18th century a byword for violence and unpredictability was The Edinburgh what?

a	Mob	b	Gang
c	Shower	d	Radges

17 The tradition of emptying chamber pots out of multi-storey buildings was preceded by which cry?

a	Gardey Loo	b	Awa wey ye
c	Oot ma' rod	d	Duck yer heid

18 What would pedestrians hastily shout out from below?

a	Haud yer haun	b	Haud yer horses
c	Haud yer bucket	d	Haud yer pail

19 Marjory Kennedy-Fraser devoted much of her life to collecting and preserving what?

a	Jam	b	Gaelic songs
c	Scottish insects	d	Ancient jokes

20 What culinary landmark first opened in Chambers Street in the 1930s?

a	A Chinese restaurant	b	A pizzeria
c	A hamburger van	d	A kebab shop

21 What was a tulzie?

a	A large fight	b	A kiss
c	A cuddle	d	A name for someone who is drunk

22 What could be found inside Anchor Close, and gave the close its name?

a	The Anchor Pub	b	An anchor maker's
c	A butter manufacturer's	d	A huge anchor

23 What character leads the famous Beltane Procession?

a	The Red Devil	b	The Green Man
c	The White Maiden	d	The Blue Nun

24 The firm Macsween is famous for making what?

a	Bagpipes	b	Kilts
c	Golf Clubs	d	Haggis

25 What were gundies?

a	Net menders	b	Sweets
c	Piles	d	High pavements

26 Edinburgh may well be named after which Northumbrian king?

a	Edwin of Deira	b	Edmund the Red
c	Edward De Briens	d	Black Edrick

27 What marked the limit of the Holyrood sanctuary for debtors?

a	The Canongate Well	b	The Watergate Circle
c	The Friar's Nook	d	The Girth Cross

28 What were the debtors hiding in Holyrood sanctuary known as?

a	The Ne'er Do Wells	b	The Abbey Lairds
c	The Loose Cannons	d	The Quiet Men

29 What was on the Burgh of Leith coat of arms?

a	The Virgin and Child	b	A tea clipper
c	A grain store	d	Neptune's horn

30 From where did the alleyways called 'closes' derive their name?

a	The heat from the tightly packed buildings	b	The word 'enclosure'
c	Many closed at 10pm	d	The buildings were close together

31 You do not have to pay an entry fee to Edinburgh Castle if you only want to visit what?

a	The Stone of Scone	b	St Margaret's Chapel
c	The restaurant	d	The National War Memorial

32 The one o'clock gun was established for what purpose?

a	To frighten tourists	b	To alert workers that it was time for lunch
c	To give an accurate time check to the trains at Waverley Station	d	To give an accurate time check to the ships in Leith Harbour

33 What's interesting about the steps leading to Calton Road from the Black Bull pub?

a	Ewan MacGregor ran down them in *Trainspotting*	b	Walking down them is said to bring good luck
c	Robert Burns wrote a poem sitting on them	d	They date back to the 12th century

34 Every summer half-naked men and women parade through South Queensferry before plunging into the cold waters of the Forth. What's this tradition called?

a	The Loony Dook	b	The Plonkers Plunge
c	The Dinky Dip	d	The Fife Dive

35 The opening lines of which writer's 'Address to Edinburgh' are 'Edina, Scotia's darling seat'?

a	George IV	b	Bonnie Prince Charlie
c	Robert Burns	d	J.K. Rowling

36 By what name would older generations of Edinburgh and Leith remember the Northern General Hospital?

a	Leith Public Health Hospital	b	Royal Infirmary
c	Western General	d	Royal Hospital

37 The Newhaven Fishing Fleet was commonly referred to as what?

a	The Reaper of the Seas	b	The Pirates of Portobello
c	The Newhaven Armada	d	The Scourge of the Ocean

38 What, in local government circles, was known as the 'Greetin' Meetin"?

a	The last meeting before the elections	b	The first meeting before the elections
c	A meeting with the Prime Minister	d	A meeting with local police

39 Which famous Edinburgh firm was known by the popular name 'The Dummie'?

a	Edinburgh and Dumfriesshire Dairy Co. Ltd	b	Kwik-Fit
c	Lothian Buses	d	Jenners

40 When were newspaper reporters first admitted to town council meetings?

a	1775	b	1820
c	1833	d	They always have been

41 Why did Edinburghers name Alan Ramsay's house on Calton Hill 'Goose Pie'?

a	Because of its shape	b	Ramsay was web-footed
c	He kept a pet goose in his garden	d	No reason

42 Can you describe a bell penny?

a	Money put aside for a wedding	b	Money put aside for a funeral
c	Money kept for a rainy day	d	Money kept for the tax board

43 The lone piper is a traditional and popular feature at the Tattoo. In which year did the first-ever woman, Officer Cadet Elaine Marnoch, take on this role?

a	1948	b	1969
c	1977	d	2001

44 What was referred to as a 'deid-chalk'?

a	A meal eaten by officers after an execution	b	A meal eaten by officers before an execution
c	Money given to officers witnessing an execution	d	Money taken from a criminal before execution

45 What was composed in a London Street house in 1874?

a	The Scottish national anthem	b	The English national anthem
c	The Icelandic national anthem	d	The German national anthem

46 Local firm McVitie & Price were famed for their wedding cakes. For whom did they bake one in 1947?

a	Princess Elizabeth and Prince Philip	**b**	Fred Astaire and Ginger Rogers
c	Winston Churchill	**d**	General Eisenhower

47 What was known as The Presbytery?

a	A club which met in Anchor Close	**b**	A social meeting hall for Church ministers
c	A coffee-house open only to politicians	**d**	A sewing circle for council workers' wives

48 Traditionally, two city churches receive Christmas trees from the Queen. St Giles is one, but what is the other?

a	St John's	**b**	St Cuthbert's
c	Canongate	**d**	St. Mary's

49 What marks the closing of the Edinburgh International Festival?

a	A parade of performers	**b**	The one o'clock gun goes off at midnight
c	A funfair in Princes Street Gardens	**d**	A fireworks concert

50 The Latin term 'Nisi Dominus Frustra' is based on a passage from Psalm 127. Who uses it as their motto?

a	City of Edinburgh	**b**	The people of Leith
c	The Scottish Parliament	**d**	Edinburgh International Festival

7

Weird Edinburgh

'Lift the sneck and draw the bar:
Bluidie Mackinye, come out if ye daur!'

Rhyme shouted by schoolboys into the Mausoleum of Sir George Mackenzie

On the surface, Edinburgh is a distinguished, urbane, well-bred city – an upstanding lady of august elegance and authority. But, behind this innocent façade, lies a darker, sleazier and creepier side of the city.

Edinburgh has (on ratio) more sex shops than anywhere else in Britain – bar London – and was also home to the UK's first cannabis cafe. Even if the latter went up in smoke, closed down by Lothian and Borders finest, after just one day. And with graveyard tours, haunted theatres and poltergeists, it is no wonder that thousands of people come to Edinburgh to be spooked by the city's ghosts, ghouls and gruesome tales.

Over the next few pages, you will discover Scotland Street tunnel's link with the Milky Way, where you can go swimming naked and what happens when you get too close to traffic cones.

1 Diane's Pool Hall had the first L-shaped what in Britain?

a	Pool table	b	Pool cue
c	Bar	d	Barmaid

2 What is the nickname given to the area dominated by lap-dancing strip bars?

a	Pubic Triangle	b	Slippery Nipple
c	The Strip	d	Seedy Circuit

3 Stolen traffic cones cost taxpayers in the capital thousands of pounds each year. How many are estimated missing per year?

a	10,000	b	500
c	2,000	d	100,000

4 Which swimming pool has nude-bathing sessions?

a	Leith Victoria	b	Dalry
c	Portobello	d	Drum Brae

5 What marks the spot of the last public hanging in Edinburgh?

a	A monument	b	A painting
c	An 'H' made of steel	d	An 'X' made of iron

6 What else does Broughton Street chip shop Piccante moonlight as?

a	A night-club with DJs	b	A taxi office
c	A private investigator's	d	A strip bar

7 A man was once charged by police for attempting to make love in public to what?

a	A rubbish bin	b	A car exhaust
c	A shoe	d	A traffic cone

8 The Great Lafayette haunts which Edinburgh theatre?

a	The Kings	b	The Playhouse
c	The Lyceum	d	The Festival Theatre

9 And how did the Great Lafayette die?

a	He fell off the stage and broke his neck	b	He fell over the railing in the upper circle
c	He died in a fire that started while he was on stage	d	He choked on his sword as he tried to swallow it

10 The Mackenzie Poltergeist is said to haunt which Edinburgh site?

a	Greyfriars Graveyard	b	The Vaults
c	The City Café	d	Mary King's Close

11 To clean grass from the cobbles in Charlotte Square the unemployed used to be given what?

a	One slice of bread	b	A goat
c	Scissors	d	Theatre tickets

12 Which four-legged film star was photographed on the stairway of the Caledonian Hotel?

a	Lassie	b	Rin-Tin-Tin
c	Mr Ed	d	Trigger

13 What was Edinburgh's fad for building railway lines in the early 18th century called?

a	Railways Galore	b	Railway Mania
c	Train Crazy	d	Sleepers a-go-go

14 Witchery tour guides are dressed as which notorious highwayman?

a	Adam Lyal	b	The Headless Horseman
c	Dick Turpin	d	Robin Hood

15 According to legend the remnants of which notorious gang died in a shoot-out with police in Leith?

a	The Ned Kelly Gang	b	The Dalton Gang
c	The Youngers	d	The James Gang

16 Dr Richard Wiseman led the world's biggest scientific ghost hunt in the South Bridge Vaults in 2002. What was his conclusion?

a	It was too dark to measure anything	**b**	The 'ghosts' were imaginary
c	The place was haunted	**d**	He should change profession

17 What were installed on the North Bridge, until repeated vandalism forced their removal?

a	Samaritan telephone help lines	**b**	Water fountains
c	Electronic maps of Edinburgh city centre	**d**	Police Boxes

18 The Scotland Street tunnel was once used to investigate what?

a	Badgers' breeding patterns	**b**	Material from space
c	Treasonable crimes	**d**	Sensory deprivation

19 There is a diary in the Royal Mile Police Museum made of what?

a	Solid silver	**b**	Recycled effluence
c	Smoked ham	**d**	Human skin

20 What is unusual about Edinburgh Zoo's only elephant?

a	It's totally deaf	**b**	It's an albino
c	It's only 8 feet high	**d**	It's a statue

21 Which 17th-century book gave Mary King's Close its terrible reputation?

a	*The Town below the Ground*	b	*Satan's Invisible World*
c	*The Wynd from Hell*	d	*The Diary of Thomas Coltheart*

22 Before it was stolen, in what odd place was one of the Forth Rail Bridge rivets displayed?

a	Harry Ramsden's chip shop	b	Jenners' restaurant
c	The Central Library men's toilet	d	Above the cigarette machine in the Vine Bar

23 How did the Duchess of Gordon raise a Scottish regiment?

a	By kissing each new recruit	b	By paying each recruit 3 shillings
c	By disguising herself as a sergeant	d	By personally declaring war on England

24 What is unusual about the Marquis of Montrose's signature on the National Covenant?

a	It's misspelled	b	It appears to be written in blood
c	The Marquis was in France when it was signed	d	Montrose was illiterate

25 What did residents of Roseburn do when they heard the rumour that a WW2 German bomber had hit the brewery on Russell Road?

a	They poured into the streets with empty jugs	b	They evacuated
c	They hid what alcohol they had left in the house	d	They looted the brewery

26 By 1700 there were how many wigmakers in Edinburgh?

a	100	b	200
c	15	d	65

27 In 1842 Edinburgh had 200 what?

a	Pubs	b	Brothels
c	Hangings	d	Prostitutes

28 One of the most popular shows at the Fringe is called 'Puppetry of the' what?

a	Balloons	b	Fingers
c	Toes	d	Penis

29 Why did goldsmith Alistir Tait alter the Church of Scotland's 'Moderator's Ring' in 2004?

a	To fit the finger of the first woman Moderator	b	The Moderator's fingers were too fat
c	The Moderator wanted to wear the ring on his pinky	d	It looked too much like a wedding ring

30 Council chiefs rapped the Burke & Hare lap-dancing bar in May 2004. Why?

a	The exterior was painted silver and black	b	It banned council employees from entering the establishment
c	The windows allowed pedestrians to see in	d	The bar wanted to allow 'al fresco' lap dancing

31 An image of Sir Walter Scott once advertised which product on an enamelled tin sign on Blair Street?

a	Shortbread	b	Cigarettes
c	Fountain pens	d	Beer

32 Who is said to haunt the White Hart Inn in the Grassmarket?

a	Deacon Brodie	b	Burke and Hare
c	Robert Burns	d	Greyfriars Bobby

33 'X-Rayed Edinburgh' adorned badges given out to those who partook in the campaign against which disease in the 1950s?

a	Meningitis	b	Cancer
c	Hepatitis	d	TB

34 Drag queen Lily Savage made his/her Scottish debut in which bar?

a	Laughing Duck	b	Ryan's
c	City Café	d	Phoenix Basement Bar

35 Why, during medieval times, were steps to some Edinburgh houses deliberately made of varying height?

a	Owing to superstition	b	So that unfamiliar 'visitors' might stumble and be heard
c	To avoid a bizarre tax law	d	It was fashionable

36 Which door can you find within the Beehive Inn on the Grassmarket?

a	A condemned cell door from Calton Jail	b	The front door of Burke and Hare's house
c	Sir Arthur Conan Doyle's study door	d	The original living-room door from Sean Connery's Fountainbridge birthplace

37 On a famous trip to Edinburgh in 1822, George IV had to retire early from a dance at the Assembly Rooms. Why?

a	It was way past his bedtime	b	He was embarrassed that he couldn't dance
c	Someone dropped his pistol on his big toe	d	He couldn't stand the music

38 There are 222,020 women in Edinburgh compared with how many men?

a	196,894	b	175,099
c	289,566	d	301,221

39 The name Rose Street is also commonly used to describe which part of many European towns?

a	Red-light districts	b	Industrial estates
c	Quarries	d	Government buildings

40 During 17th-century Edinburgh the burnt ashes of doves' dung were used to treat what?

a	Impotence	b	Toothache
c	Headaches	d	Baldness

41 What was the first animal to be bought by Edinburgh Zoo?

a	A penguin	b	A gannet
c	A rhino	d	A polar bear

42 How much did it cost?

a	18p	b	£1
c	£99	d	£101

43 Of what did Western Union once say 'it's an interesting novelty without any commercial possibilities'?

a	Graham Bell's telephone	b	Logie Baird's television
c	Graham Bell's fax	d	Inglis Ker's proposal for a bridge to be built across the Forth

44 'The Flowers of Scotland' was a popular nickname for the stench that emanated from the sewers between tenements. Where did the name originate?

a	In a poem	b	In a book
c	In a fiddle tune	d	In a film

45 In Broxburn, West Lothian, what became a bizarre tourist attraction at the turn of the 20th century?

a	A 100 foot-long icicle formed on the Union Canal	b	A tree shaped like a man
c	A crater left by an alien space ship	d	The ditch into which Robert Burns apparently fell shortly before he died

46 What was produced to mark the phenomenon?

a	A monument	b	A plaque
c	A postcard	d	A neon sign

47 Why, for a time in the 1700s, did magistrates order the slaughter of all dogs?

a	A butcher's dog went mad	b	Witches put demonic spells on them
c	Eating dogs made you look younger	d	They carried a rare life-threatening virus

48 An ancient privilege of the doorkeepers at the Court of Session is to demand a 5-shilling penalty from any noisy individual who wears what?

a	Spurs	b	Ear rings
c	Slippers	d	Tattoos

49 On average, how many hours of bright sunshine does Edinburgh receive a year?

a	1351	b	None
c	5411	d	3009

50 How much will it cost you to have City of Edinburgh Council provide you with a weekday burial and lair?

a	£955	b	£1,010
c	£1,233	d	£2,000

8

The Arts

Edinburgh, as everyone knows, is a hot bed of artistic flair. Every day, creative types are drawn to Edinburgh like metal fillings to a magnet. From writers to dancers to graffiti artists – the city is awash with accomplished craftsmanship. From Irvine Welsh's Muirhouse through to Sean Connery's Fountainbridge, Edinburgh has the ability to forge genuine talent.

Nearly every corner shop displays an advert to join a band, make a film or write a piece of poetry. At the Cameo Cinemas, The Blue Room has launched the careers of many a young filmmaker. Performance poetry club, Big Word, has reinvented the way people think about rhyme and verse. And, with live music thriving seven nights a week, we're now in a position where there are more bands than there are audiences.

Every August thousands of performers and visitors descend on Edinburgh for the world's largest arts festival, which has been running since the 1940s. There is something for everyone, from world-class opera and drama to street performers and cross-dressing cabaret. Shows come in all shapes and sizes, with Hollywood stars and young hopefuls rubbing shoulders. And venues range from the backseat of a Jaguar to the opulence of the Usher Hall.

Still not convinced? Look up arts in the dictionary and you just might find a picture of Edinburgh there instead of a definition.

1 Author Irvine Welsh is most famous for which book?

a	*Trainspotting*	b	*The Crow Road*
c	Harry Potter series	d	Inspector Rebus series

2 There are several statues of which animals at the top of Leith Walk

a	Pigeons	b	Squirrels
c	Cats	d	Frogs

3 Who used to perform weekly at Clowns Bar?

a	Nazareth	b	Buddy Bud and the Buddy Bud Buds
c	The Proclaimers	d	Tam White and the Dexters

4 What inspired Dickens's *Christmas Carol*?

a	Everyone in Edinburgh.	b	The ghost of Queensferry House
c	The headstone of Ebenezer Scroggie	d	Geese at Duddingstone Loch

5 Peter Cook, Dudley Moore, Alan Bennett and Jonathan Millar made up which Festival comedy team?

a	That Was the Week That Was	b	Beyond the Fringe
c	The original Monty Python	d	The Cambridge Footlights

6 Where is the Edinburgh Book Festival traditionally held?

a	Charlotte Square	b	The Meadows
c	Trunks Close	d	Holyrood Park

7 Who is the Morningside cat made famous in a series of children's books?

a	Maisie	b	Garfield
c	Tom	d	Fluff

8 Muriel Spark's Miss Jean Brodie was modelled on Christina Kay. Who was she?

a	Her brother's wife	b	Her next-door neighbour
c	Her aunt	d	Her teacher

9 What famous author drinks in the Oxford Bar?

a	Ian Rankin	b	Ian Banks
c	Irvine Welsh	d	J.K. Rowling

10 What was the name of the female lead singer of the band The Rezillos?

a	June Troon	b	Faye Fife
c	Kerry Oot	d	Lee Thwock

11 What was the name of Edinburgh's first performance poetry club?

| a | The Living Word | b | The Big Word |
| c | Poet Jam | d | Poets Anonymous |

12 In the 19th century John Kay was famous in Edinburgh for producing what?

| a | Caricatures | b | Wax statues |
| c | Stuffed animals | d | Cartoons |

13 For which subject was the sculptor Sir John Steell the most famous in Britain?

| a | Nudes | b | Royalty |
| c | Military men | d | Horses |

14 What was the most famous work of the poet Alan Ramsay?

| a | 'The Exciseman' | b | 'The Westpans Kelpie' |
| c | 'The Gentle Shepherd' | d | 'The Ballad of Hopetoun House' |

15 What was the 19th-century writer Susan Ferrier known as?

| a | Edinburgh's Catherine Cookson | b | Scotland's Jane Austen |
| c | The Abbeyhill Scribe | d | The Last Jacobite |

16 Where was the Scottish Book Trust headquarters before moving to Trunk's Close?

a	Above Fountainbridge Library	**b**	Coburg Street
c	The Calton Studio	**d**	The Writers' Museum

17 Which one of these was *not* discovered at the Festival Fringe?

a	Rowan Atkinson	**b**	Ben Elton
c	Rory Bremner	**d**	Fry and Laurie

18 Which of these works did author John Gay write?

a	*The Beggar's Opera*	**b**	*The Tinker's Tale*
c	*The People's Poet*	**d**	*The Emperor's New Clothes*

19 What is Jack Vettriano's best-known painting?

a	*The Dancing Waiter*	**b**	*The Singing Butler*
c	*The Dumb Waiter*	**d**	*Umbrellas at Dawn*

20 T.S. Eliot's famous poems inspired the musical *Cats*, what were they based on?

a	Kay's cartoons	**b**	The Edinburgh cat sanctuary
c	His landlady's pussy	**d**	Stray cats in Greyfriars

21 Which famous Scottish violinist was painted by Sir Henry Raeburn?

a	Niel Gow	b	Angus Cameron
c	William Gerber	d	Silas Gumm

22 Who carved the large rounded sculptures in the gardens of the Gallery of Modern Art?

a	Henry Moore	b	Rennie MacIntosh
c	Patrick Geddes	d	Robert Adam

23 What was architect Sir Basil Spence's most famous and controversial design?

a	Liverpool Cathedral	b	The Dresden Fraukirke
c	Coventry Cathedral	d	The Angel of the North

24 The artist Phoebe Traquair was Edinburgh's most acclaimed exponent of which style?

a	Art Deco	b	Art Nouveau
c	Deconstructionism	d	Cubism

25 In the statue in the City Chambers Courtyard what is the name of the horse that Alexander is wrestling?

a	Sheba	b	Bucepheles
c	West Tip	d	Siskin

26 What was Rab in John Brown's book *Rab and His Friends*?

a	A priest	b	An invisible friend
c	A mastiff	d	A tailor

27 What was the painter Alexander Nasmyth known as?

a	Father of the Edinburgh Landscape	b	Father of the Scottish Landscape
c	King of Scottish Watercolours	d	Chief of the Lothian Landscape

28 Who was the first director of the Edinburgh Festival?

a	Rudolph Bing	b	Jim Poole
c	Paul Gudgin	d	Rikki Fulton

29 Which now-famous poet was born and died in poverty in the Cowgate?

a	William McGonagall	b	Norman McCaig
c	Edwin Muir	d	Robert Tannahill

30 Who *hasn't* appeared at Murrayfield Stadium?

a	Robbie Williams	b	The Pope
c	David Bowie	d	Cliff Richard

31 What first hit Edinburgh's streets on 25 June 1993?

a	The first Scottish *Big Issue*	**b**	Fopp Record Shop's first stall
c	Greenways bus lanes	**d**	The *Scotsman/Edinburgh Evening News* news stalls

32 Which folk singer was also an art teacher at St Serfs?

a	Barbara Dickson	**b**	Donnie Munroe
c	Tam White	**d**	Jim Sutherland

33 Edinburgh and Kirriemuir have Britain's only two working examples of what?

a	Mechanical Peter Pan models	**b**	Camera Obscuras
c	'Maiden' Guillotines	**d**	Victorian Reiger church organs

34 Who designed the giant 'foot' outside St Mary's Cathedral?

a	Eduardo Paolozzi	**b**	Frank Gehry
c	Krausekrause	**d**	Terry Farrell

35 The musician Matthew Hardie was known as what?

a	The Scottish Stravinski	**b**	The Scottish Stradivari
c	The Caledonian Verdi	**d**	Scotland's Beethoven

36 Who persuaded Robert Louis Stevenson to make Dr Jekyll and Mr Hyde the same person?

a	His wife	**b**	His doctor
c	His next door neighbour	**d**	His local barman

37 Sir Harry Lauder was the first British artist to do what?

a	Sell a million records	**b**	Appear on Top of the Pops
c	Receive a platinum disc	**d**	Have two songs in the Top Ten

38 Which famous phrase was invented by Robert Louis Stevenson?

a	The Land of Make Believe	**b**	The Land of Nod
c	And They Lived Happily Ever After	**d**	Home Is Where the Heart Is

39 Which well-known author was born in Castle Street in 1859?

a	Kenneth Grahame	**b**	James Barrie
c	John Buchan	**d**	Compton Mackenzie

40 Who wrote the original book *Greyfriars Bobby*?

a	Eleanor Atkinson	**b**	Enid Blyton
c	Roald Dahl	**d**	Robert Louis Stevenson

41 Which cartoon superhero battled a villain on Edinburgh Castle's ramparts in a famous episode of his comic

a	Spiderman	b	Superman
c	Batman	d	Captain America

42 Where would you find sculptures of a group of chickens?

a	Fountainpark	b	Kinnaird Park
c	Murrayfield Stadium	d	St James Centre

43 Guarding Edinburgh Zoo's old gatehouse are statues of what?

a	Bronze tigers	b	Killer whales
c	Pandas	d	Golden Eagles

44 Who paid for the poet Robert Fergusson's headstone?

a	Bonnie Prince Charlie	b	Robert Burns
c	Sir Walter Scott	d	Robert Louis Stevenson

45 What was Edinburgh's famous punk band called?

a	The Exploited	b	Discrepancy
c	Gamma vs Delta	d	Dejecta

46 Anthony Daniels opened the Star Wars exhibition at the Market Street Art Exhibition Centre in 2001. Which character did he play in the saga?

a	R2D2	b	Darth Vader
c	C3PO	d	One of the cuddly Ewoks

47 Which Edinburgh publisher first printed Irvine Welsh's *Trainspotting*?

a	Black & White	b	Rebel Inc.
c	Canongate Books	d	Chapman

48 At the 2003 MTV Europe Awards held in Leith, which act was introduced flying over Edinburgh in a computer-generated spaceship?

a	Michael Jackson	b	Justin Timberlake
c	The Darkness	d	Christine Aguilera

49 Founded by Mike Hart, the jazz festival is the longest-running in the country. In which year was it founded?

a	1960	b	1939
c	1978	d	1988

50 DCC Bob Skinner has investigated many crimes in Edinburgh. But who is his creator?

a	Quintin Jardine	b	Ruth Rendell
c	Ian Rankin	d	Patricia Cornwell

9

Leading and Lagging

'City of everywhere, broken
necklace in the sun,
you are caves of guilt, you are
pinnacles of jubliation.'

Norman McCaig

Glasgow Smiles Better? It had a successful Garden Festival, was European City of Culture and is the friendliest city in the world. In fact, things were looking pretty good for our friendly neighbours, the Weegies – for a while.

But, in 2004, Edinburgh has the jobs, the food, the arts, the style, the gardens and the architectural elegance. She also has a royal yacht, the largest arts festival in the world and the two biggest tourist attractions in the country – and, for those just back from Mars, the Scottish Parliament, too.

Things aren't always so good, though. The traffic situation makes rush hour in New York look like a leisurely Sunday drive and financial blunders have raised serious questions about the aforementioned Scottish Parliament.

But, Edinburgh has plenty to be proud of. The Forth Rail Bridge is one of the great wonders of the world and Edinburgh has consistently led the way – medically and mechanically – to better our way of life. How many other cities can you say that about?

1 Edinburgh's Hogmanay celebrations were cancelled on New Year's Eve 2003. What was the official reason for postponing the event?

a	Bad weather	b	A bomb was found under a drain in Princes Street
c	Glasgow was the place to be	d	Overcrowding in the city centre

2 What name was given to the new cloned sheep at the Roslin Institute near the city?

a	Barbara	b	Milly
c	Dolly	d	Flossy

3 There was an outcry when the Scottish Parliament spent an additional £663,000 so that MSPs could each have what?

a	A DVD player	b	A laptop computer
c	A widescreen TV	d	A pay rise

4 At a cost of £19,000 to the tax payer Parliament bosses have also fitted MSPs' offices with which item?

a	Cooker	b	Microwave
c	Fridge	d	Cable TV

5 In the 1970s, trains took 43 minutes to go from Glasgow Central to Waverley Station. How long is the average journey now?

a	39 minutes	b	41 minutes
c	50 minutes	d	60 minutes

6 Which of these did *not* go to Edinburgh University Medical School?

a	Sir Arthur Conan Doyle	b	Joseph Lister
c	W.C. Grace	d	Charles Darwin

7 Who wrote what is now regarded as the first published theory of evolution?

a	Charles Darwin	b	Alfred Wallace
c	James Burnett	d	Lord Greystoke

8 James Young Simpson was a pioneer of which medical marvel?

a	Penicillin	b	Chloroform
c	Aspirin	d	Paracetamol

9 Which of these was *not* on display at Ingliston's Classic Car Museum?

a	The Batmobile	b	Basil Fawlty's Mini
c	The Love Bug	d	Kitt from *Knight Rider*

10 Due to public outcry several attempts in the 1990s to build a memorial to whom were abandoned?

a	Burke and Hare	b	Every witch drowned in the Nor' Loch
c	The last man publicly hanged in 'Edinburgh	d	The Bodysnatchers

11 How much did Leith's new mini-hospital, The Leith Community Treatment Centre, cost to build?

a	£30 million	**b**	£750,000
c	£8 million	**d**	It was donated for free

12 What is the name given to Edinburgh's unique bus lanes?

a	Betterways	**b**	Greenways
c	Highways	**d**	Lateways

13 The Forth Railway Bridge is known as the what 'Wonder of the World'?

a	Fifth	**b**	Eighth
c	Seventh	**d**	Second

14 In 1862, how long did it take to travel from London to Edinburgh aboard *The Flying Scotsman* steam train?

a	10-and-a-half hours	**b**	A day
c	48 hours	**d**	5 hours

15 The 18th century is known in Edinburgh as the 'Age of ' what?

a	Decadence	**b**	Improvement
c	Progress	**d**	Prosperity

16 Which new Edinburgh festival recently attracted 1,500 visitors from as far away as Germany and America?'

a	The Dark City Goth Festival	b	The European Punk Fest
c	Edinburgh Country & Western Festival	d	MELA

17 The City of Edinburgh Car-Free Festival cost the taxpayer £100,000. What did city leader Donald Anderson call it?

a	A success	b	A waste of money
c	A scam	d	A gimmick

18 Which Edinburgh hotel won the 2004 Scottish Hotel Restaurant of the Year award?

a	Point Hotel	b	Apex Hotel
c	Balmoral Hotel	d	Roxburghe Hotel

19 Edinburgh could soon be hosting the qualifying events and training camps for which prestigious event?

a	British Grand Prix	b	2012 Olympic Games
c	Wimbledon	d	U21 Football World Cup

20 Edinburgh Castle was the nation's top paid-for tourist attraction in 2004. What came second?

a	Edinburgh National Gallery	b	Edinburgh Zoo
c	Holyrood Palace	d	Stirling Castle

21 How will new buses running between Edinburgh Castle and Holyrood Palace be powered?

a	Steam	b	Solar Power
c	Battery	d	Electricity

22 What opened in 1507 at the foot of Blackfriars Wynd, and was the very first in Scotland?

a	Kilt shop	b	Printing press
c	Coffee house	d	Swimming pool

23 The first anti-tobacco tract – Counterblast Against Tobacco – was written by whom?

a	Robert Burns	b	John Knox
c	Deacon Brodie	d	James VI

24 Edinburgh is bidding to become a UNESCO-designated World City of what?

a	Literature	b	Architecture
c	Fashion	d	Sport

25 Today, the North Bridge can carry a vehicle weighing up to how many tonnes?

a	10	b	40
c	55	d	100

26 It was estimated that the Forth Road Bridge would cost 3 million pounds. How much was the eventual bill?

a	5 million	**b**	10 million
c	19 million	**d**	1 billion

27 How wide is the Forth Road Bridge?

a	58 feet	**b**	33 feet
c	30 metres	**d**	50 metres

28 What excuse was given for taking nine years to complete the building of the George IV Bridge?

a	Lack of funds	**b**	There weren't enough labourers
c	It was cursed by witches	**d**	They wanted to take their time

29 The Midlothian County Council once demolished an entire street to make way for its offices. Which street was it?

a	Great Junction Street	**b**	Niddrie Street
c	Lothian Street	**d**	Melbourne Street

30 What took 3 years and a quarter of a million pounds to complete?

a	Edinburgh–Glasgow railway line	**b**	Scottish Executive's car park
c	Hearts stadium's Gorgie Stand	**d**	Commonwealth Pool

31 George Chalmers financed the Chalmers Hospital with £30,000 of his own money. What was his occupation?

a	Vet	b	Doctor
c	Plumber	d	Architect

32 The Playfair Project opened in August 2004, providing a link between which two buildings?

a	The National Gallery of Scotland and the Portrait Gallery	b	The Portrait Gallery and the Royal Scottish Academy
c	The Royal Scottish Academy and the Gallery of Modern Art	d	The National Gallery and the Royal Scottish Academy

33 According to the Royal National Institute of the Blind, how many Edinburgh firms said it would be difficult or impossible to employ someone partially sighted or blind?

a	0 out of 10	b	2 out of 10
c	6 out of 10	d	9 out of 10

34 Those who didn't pay their 'poor rates' in 1894 wouldn't have been able to what?

a	Apply for a bank account	b	Vote
c	Leave the country	d	Obtain a passport

35 With each of its 48 rooms fitted with PC, DVD and Hi-Fi, the Bonham Hotel is staking a claim to the title of the 'World's Most' what 'Guest House'?

a	Technological	b	Wired
c	Electric	d	Tuned In

36 Charles Higham described Edinburgh as a 'dignified spinster with' what?

a	Dark secrets	b	Unsightly nose hair
c	Fleas	d	Syphilis

37 Edinburgh has a high ratio of accountants. How many are there registered at present?

a	999	b	1322
c	2500	d	20,000

38 The troubled Scottish Parliament superseded its original estimated cost of £30 million. What was the final estimated cost?

a	£300 million	b	£431 million
c	£1 billion	d	£48 million

39 Leading architect Andrew Doolan won a Royal Institute of British Architects award for Dick House. Where in town can it be found?

a	The Shore	b	Bread Street
c	The Grange	d	Melbourne Place

40 What will cost £1 billion and have towers constructed from reinforced concrete?

a	A new transport bridge to be built to the west of the Forth Road Bridge	b	A new state-of-the-art sporting arena in Sighthill
c	A new airport built in West Lothian	d	A replacement for the current Forth Rail Bridge

41 The council's controversial road tolls are estimated to cost £429 million. But how much will it cost to cross its cordons into the city?

a	50p	b	£2
c	£3.50	d	£5

42 Which club was forced to make way for the City of Edinburgh Council's new home in New Street?

a	The Poets Club	b	The Archers Club
c	The Bongo Club	d	The Comedy Club

43 Sir Patrick Geddes created plans for over 20 cities in India as well as for Edinburgh. Where will a new glass sculpture of him be situated?

a	Outside the new council head-quarters on East Market Street	b	In the foyer of the new Scottish Parliament
c	Inside Edinburgh Castle	d	On top of Calton Hill

44 A new civic square in the heart of Munich is to be named after Edinburgh to mark 50 years of friendship between the two cities. What will it be called?

a	Von Edinburgher	b	Da Edinbourgitz
c	Von Dina burgh	d	The Edinburghplatz

45 Days after announcing the closure of Fountainbridge Brewery, Scottish and Newcastle's yearly profit was revealed as how much?

a	£47 million	b	£471 million
c	£147 million	d	£741 million

46 Chloroform looked set to remain a local medical fad until what happened?

a	Queen Victoria started using it	b	It was sold to America
c	The Archbishop of Canterbury blessed it	d	King George ordered it be made nationally available

47 How many murders was the mass killer William Burke finally convicted of?

a	One	b	Three
c	Nine	d	11

48 James Rutherford was the inventor of what?

a	Electricity	b	The light bulb
c	The gas lamp	d	The reusable match

49 In 1842 Thomas Sturrock and Charles Drummond invented what?

a	The Christmas card	b	Steak and gravy pies
c	The stapler	d	The accordion

50 James Hutton is known as the father of what?

a	Motor racing	b	Geology
c	Hair styling	d	Town planning

10
Miscellaneous

As we draw to a close, we'd like to dedicate the last chapter to all those awkward bits 'n' bobs that didn't seem to fit anywhere else. The leftovers, the oily remnants, the spare parts. Oddities that have no particular home of their own – a bit like the regulars who drink in Leith Walk's many bars, you might say.

There's plenty here to keep you entertained – and perplexed. (No, we're not talking about a day trip to Ocean Terminal.) Lou Reed, Russian bars and silver-painted street entertainers, they've all squeezed their way in somehow. And, if you're lucky, perhaps Kurt Cobain and bus-robbing bandits will put in an appearance, too.

1 Complete the phrase Glaswegians often use to describe Edinburghers: 'All fur coat and nae' what?

a	Thong	b	Pants
c	Drawers	d	Knickers

2 What is the name of the popular Fringe theatre venue that was once a mental institution?

a	Mental	b	Bedlam
c	Crackers	d	Fruit Looper

3 Edinburgh Zoo is renowned for which animals?

a	Penguins	b	Tigers
c	Pandas	d	Rhinos

4 What's unique about the bar Fingers in Frederick Street?

a	It's Edinburgh's only official piano bar	b	It's strictly a singles-only bar
c	It doesn't serve alcohol	d	You aren't allowed in unless you're wearing trainers

5 Edinburgh's only Russian bar is called Da Da Da. What does it mean in English?

a	No No No	b	Yes Yes Yes
c	OK OK OK	d	Drink Drink Drink

6 Harry Potter author J.K. Rowling used to write about the boy wizard from which coffee house?

a	The Elephant House	b	Beanscene
c	Café Politik	d	Royal Mile Starbucks

7 The *Scotsman* newspaper once published a review of a rock show that never took place. Which artist was in question?

a	Bon Jovi	b	Frank Zappa
c	Michael Jackson	d	Meat Loaf

8 How many monarchs have landed at Leith?

a	None	b	Three
c	Five	d	Ten

9 People flock to Edinburgh to study at its universities. Approximately how many students are there?

a	33,500	b	57,000
c	100,100	d	Too many

10 Which city did Robert Louis Stevenson say Edinburgh ought to be like?

a	Glasgow	b	London
c	Paris	d	New York

11 Environmental visitor centre Dynamic Earth's slogan maintains you can live how many 'million years in one day'?

a	500	b	1,000
c	1,500	d	2,400

12 The Water of Leith is how many miles long?

a	15	b	22
c	28	d	38

13 Leith pipped Edinburgh to open which shop first?

a	Co-op supermarket	b	HMV
c	Woolworths	d	Marks & Spencer

14 Where did Sir Walter Scott find Edinburgh's missing crown jewels?

a	In a cache on Arthur's Seat	b	In a chest in Edinburgh Castle
c	In a drawer in Holyrood Palace	d	Buried in a shallow grave on Calton Hill

15 What is different about the 'E' and 'U' in the City of Edinburgh Council's logo?

a	The size	b	The colour
c	There is no difference	d	The shape

16 According to lore, what did the devil predict from the steps of the Mercat Cross?

a	The plague	b	The battle of Flodden
c	WW1	d	The death of James VI

17 What was Scotland's largest street brawl called?

a	The Cleansing of the Causeway	b	The Tollcross Tulzie
c	The Stramash of Stockbridge	d	The Demolition of Merchiston Gate

18 What in Edinburgh Castle is 110 feet deep?

a	The Castle well	b	The Castle's Dungeon Keep
c	The moat	d	The Castle's ammunition reserve

19 What was used to secure a fresh body so that it couldn't be stolen?

a	Mortice locks	b	Superglue
c	Re-enforced concrete	d	9-inch nails

20 What were the Pickwick, the Owl and the Waverley?

a	Pubs	b	Pens
c	Train stations	d	Markets

21 Who does the statue outside the Sheraton Hotel reputedly represent?

a	Pearl Bailey	b	Ariel Williams Holloway
c	Josephine Baker	d	Winnie Mandela

22 What is confusing about the statue of Sir Walter Scott in Parliament Square?

a	It's not the famous writer	b	He appears to be sleeping
c	It's a woman	d	The statue has two left hands and feet

23 One is lying down outside Leith Theatre while another pushes a barrel. They are statues of what?

a	Pirates	b	Sailors
c	Coopers	d	Fishwives

24 While staying at the Balmoral Hotel, Velvet Underground singer, Lou Reed, sent a drink back nine times because they couldn't make it 'taste right.' What type of drink was it?

a	Tea	b	Coffee
c	Vodka and Red Bull	d	Banana milkshake

25 Derek Dick is one of Edinburgh's most famous rock singers. By what name is he better known?

a	Frog	b	Fish
c	Elvis	d	Bono

26 Brightly patterned squares on certain Lothian Buses are based on a Versace dress worn by which Hollywood actress?

a	Nicole Kidman	b	Liz Hurley
c	Sandra Bullock	d	Jennifer Lopez

27 What did Green MSP Robin Harper have to dash off and purchase before being sworn into the Scottish Parliament in 1999?

a	A hat	b	A tie
c	A flower	d	A pair of glasses

28 In Irvine Walsh's *Porno*, the sequel to *Trainspotting*, from which bar does Francis Begbie finally spot his double-crossing pal, Mark Renton?

a	Swanny's	b	Tam O' Shanter
c	Port O' Leith	d	The Central Bar

29 Which film set in Edinburgh marked the debut production of Elton John's Rocket Pictures?

a	*Restless Natives*	b	*Trainspotting*
c	*Women Talking Dirty*	d	*The Debt Collector*

30 How long will public tours at the new Scottish Parliament building last?

a	One hour	b	45 minutes
c	As long as it took to build	d	All day

31 What did *Wired* magazine call The Malmaison Hotel?

a	Out-of-date	b	A glamourised Leith brothel
c	Rock 'n' roll	d	Cheap and cheerful

32 Corstorphine Hill has a radio mast, a ruined tower, and a boundary with the wild plains of Africa (at the Zoo). What else does it have that few people know about?

a	A vast redundant nuclear shelter	b	A medieval torture dungeon
c	A private underground hotel	d	A helicopter pad

33 Edinburgh's biggest gay nightclub, CC Blooms, is named after Bette Midler's character in which film?

a	*The Rose*	b	*Outrageous Fortune*
c	*Beaches*	d	*GI Jane*

34 The Dominion cinema in Morningside is Edinburgh's oldest independent cinema. What film was showing when it opened its doors for the first time on 31 January 1938?

a	*Gone With The Wind*	b	*The Wizard Of Oz*
c	*Wee Willy Winky*	d	*Way Out West*

35 Kurt Cobain once played an acoustic charity gig in Edinburgh. Where was it held?

a	Hunter Square	b	Tap O' Lauriston
c	Princes Street Gardens	d	Southsider Bar

36 What is the exact length of the Royal Mile?

a	1.25 miles	b	1.50 kilometres
c	1 mile	d	1 mile, 100 yards

37 What are the official colours of Lothian Regional Transport's buses?

a	Douche Maroon and White	b	Rose Wine and Cream
c	Burgundy and White	d	None of these

38 Which theatre staged its first West End musical, selling out a 14-week run in 1989?

a	Festival Theatre	b	Kings Theatre
c	Traverse	d	Playhouse

39 How many trains are said to pass over the Forth Rail Bridge every 24 hours?

a	50	b	95
c	165	d	200

40 What is the name of the Robert Louis Stevenson poem inscribed on a plaque outside his Heriot Row home?

a	Home Is Where The Heart Is	b	The Lamplighter
c	There And Back Again	d	Home Sweet Home

41 The Revolution night-club on Lothian Road was once home to which cinema?

a	Lothian Picture House	**b**	Caley Cinema
c	Edinburgh Moviedrome	**d**	The Starlighter

42 Jenners co-founder Charles Jenners once described Edinburgh women as 'the best' what 'in the Kingdom'?

a	Dressed	**b**	Kissers
c	Looking	**d**	Dancers

43 The clock above Frasers department store used to play music. One tune was Caller Herrin. What was the other?

a	Flower of Scotland	**b**	Auld Lang Syne
c	Scotland the Brave	**d**	Green Grass of Home

44 What is the name of the Belgian mirrored tent that has become a favourite at the Edinburgh International Book Festival?

a	The Chocolate Tent	**b**	The Tee-pee
c	The Beer Tent	**d**	The Speigeltent

45 Pop star Prince performed in Edinburgh in the early 1990s. Where was the gig held?

a	Murrayfield Stadium	**b**	Edinburgh Castle
c	Easter Road	**d**	Meadowbank Stadium

46 The Rosslyn Chapel near Edinburgh was built by William Sinclair, a grand master of the Knights Templar. What was suggested as his reasons for building it?

a	To house the maps of Atlantis	**b**	To house the Holy Grail
c	To house the Turin Shroud	**d**	To house the Dead Sea Scrolls

47 SSP Drugs Spokesman Kevin Williamson disrupted the Scottish Parliament in 2003 with a one-man protest in the public gallery. Who was he mimicking?

a	Tony Blair	**b**	Jack McConnell
c	President George W. Bush	**d**	Maggie Thatcher

48 What do Dalry Road, King's Stables Road, Morrison Street, Castle Terrace, Dewar Place Lane, Lothian Road, Torphichen Street, Torphichen Place, and Canning Street all have in common?

a	They're all streets lying above the Haymarket railway tunnel	**b**	They were all built within a week
c	None of them has a number 1 address	**d**	Each one has or had a cinema on it

49 What is Edinburgh's Fools & Heroes?

a	A fantasy live role-playing society	**b**	A swingers group
c	A comedy club	**d**	A trainspotters club

50 Street entertainer 'Silver' has been busking on Princes Street for well over 15 years. What does his act incorporate?

a	Juggling	**b**	Robotics
c	Fire-breathing	**d**	Singing

119

THE ANSWERS

1 People

1 What type of dog was Greyfriar's Bobby?
c Skye terrier

2 At which school did James Bond creator Ian Fleming study?
a Fettes College

3 Sean Connery used to be a nightclub bouncer and coffin polisher before becoming a famous actor. What other job did he have in the 1950s?
b Milkman

4 John Gibson is Edinburgh's longest serving – and oldest – newspaper columnist. Which paper does he write for?
c Edinburgh Evening News

5 Queen Street is named after which Queen?
a Queen Charlotte

6 Which great Edinburgh actor starred in the St Trinian's series as the school's headmistress and her brother?
a Alistair Sim

7 Which popular rock singer went to Broughton High School?
b Shirley Manson

8 What was Tony Blair's nickname at Fettes College?
c Millie

9 James Gillespie, founder of Gillespie's Hospital, manufactured which product?
d Snuff

10 What do Giuseppe Garibaldi, Samuel Pepys, Benjamin Franklin, the Queen Mother, Yehudi Menuhin and Sean Connery all have in common?
a They were (or are) Freemen of the City of Edinburgh

11 John Knox was mistaken for what on his return to Edinburgh in 1558?
d An Englishman

12 Which famous architect designed the National Monument on Calton Hill?
a William Henry Playfair

13 George Boyd built a wooden bridge across the Nor' Loch so people could visit his shop. What kind of shop was it?
d A tailor's

14 Charlotte Square was designed by Robert Adam. The statue inside the square is a memorial to whom?
a Prince Albert

15 Adam Smith, buried in Canongate Kirkyard, was the father of what?
b Capitalism

16 Who was Scottish Widows' most famous customer?
a Sir Walter Scott

17 What was sold by Harry Tranter with his famous sign ENGLISH SPOKEN, AMERICAN UNDERSTOOD?
a Postcards

18 What does it say on the tombstone of John Porteous?
c Murdered

19 According to legend, what was Deacon Brodie hiding in when he was arrested?
b A wardrobe

20 How did 18th-century General John Reid combat the stress of military campaigns?
c Composing flute sonatas

21 What connection does Sir Arthur Conan
Doyle's monument in Picardy Place have
with the building positioned directly
behind him?

b His mother ran a boarding house there

22 Inventor of the telephone, Alexander
Graham Bell, was born in Charlotte
Square. In which country did he die?

c Canada

23 Maggie Dickson was hanged in the
Grassmarket. On the way to her burial
how was she brought back to life?

**a By the jolting of the cart carrying
her**

24 Who was born in Portobello in 1870?

a Sir Harry Lauder

25 What did the famous geologist and
author Hugh Miller do in Portobello that
same year?

c Shoot himself

26 Which journalist and presenter was born
in Edinburgh in 1919?

b Ludovic Kennedy

27 What famous couple honeymooned in
Edinburgh in 1811?

a Percy and Mary Shelley

28 Who is the current Edinburgh Festival
Fringe Director?

c Paul Gudgin

29 In Blackfriars Street in 1506, Walter
Chepman and Andrew Mylar produced
Scotland's first what?

a Printed book

30 There is a statue of the Duke of
Wellington on a horse outside Register
House. What was his mount's name?

a Copenhagen

31 What did Dr Johnson throw out the
window of the White Horse Inn?

d His lemonade

32 Why did Queen Victoria knight Sir John
Steell?

b She liked his sculpture of her husband

33 James Braidwood founded Britain's first
what?

a Municipal Fire Department

34 What is notable about the Abraham
Lincoln statue in Calton Cemetery?

**b It was the first erected outside the
USA**

35 The poet Robert Fergusson died in the
Edinburgh Bedlam after which
unfortunate incident?

c Falling downstairs drunk

36 How old was he?

c 24

37 Which style of verse, adopted by
Robert Burns, did Fergusson make
popular?

a The Standard Habbie

38 What was Jesse King better known as?

d The Stockbridge Baby Farmer

39 Which Scots heroine went to boarding
school in Old Stamp Office Close?

b Flora MacDonald

40 What was Major Thomas Weir known as?
b   The Wizard of the West Bow

41 What was John Graham of Claverhouse known as before he became Bonnie Dundee?
d   Bluidy Claver's

42 What was Robert Burns' sweetheart, Mrs McLehose, better known as?
a   Clarinda

43 Who was removed from Edinburgh's coat of arms in 1562?
a   St Giles

44 Students of 19th-century professor and philosopher Dugald Stewart said there was 'eloquence in his very' what?
a   Spitting

45 Who is regarded as the greatest philospher to have written in the English language?
c   David Hume

46 The oldest equestrian statue in Britain, erected outside St Giles' Cathedral (1685), is of King Charles II. What is he dressed as?
a   A Roman emperor

47 In 1650, the Marquis of Montrose was publicly hanged and then dismembered in Parliament Square. Where was his head fixed on a stake?
c   On the Mercat Cross

48 Clerk Maxwell was greatly influential in the field of physics. For which discovery was he most highly regarded?
a   Microwaves

49 Famous for discovering logarithms, John Napier failed to graduate from which university?
d   St Andrews University

50 The anaesthetic properties of chloroform help control pain. Who, on 4 November 1847, invented it?
a   James Young Simpson

2 Places

1 In 2002 which popular festival venue was wiped out in a terrible fire?
a **Gilded Balloon**

2 What establishment is right above Gilmerton Cove?
a **A betting shop**

3 Sean Connery was born and raised in which area of Edinburgh?
c **Fountainbridge**

4 The Black Watch memorial at the top of Playfair Steps commemorates which war?
a **The Boer War**

5 What is the name of Edinburgh's international airport?
a **Turnhouse**

6 Where was the original location of the Scotsman newspaper's premises?
a **North Bridge**

7 What was the name of the close where Robert Burns stayed, now incorporated into Lady Stair's Close?
c **Baxter's Close**

8 What is the nickname of Edinburgh's popular gay district?
d **Pink Triangle**

9 The Revolution nightclub on Lothian Road hosted a live televised show for which popular BBC TV music programme?
c **Top of the Pops**

10 What is Musselburgh's nickname?
b **The Honest Toun**

11 What gave Portobello its name?
b **A town in Panama**

12 What was Portobello once nicknamed?
b **The Scottish Brighton**

13 When was the port of Leith incorporated into Edinburgh?
a **1920**

14 What was Newhaven's original name?
b **Our Lady's Port of Grace**

15 Why is New Street so called?
d **Because it was new**

16 Where is the Scottish Storytelling Centre?
b **Netherbow Theatre**

17 Deacon Brodie's last botched burglary was an attempt to rob what?
a **The Excise Office**

18 What is carved into the pavements of Lady Stair's Close?
a **Quotes from Scottish writers**

19 What will happen if the tree next to the Corstorphine Dovecot is cut down?
a **The owner's wife will die**

20 What is the Edinburgh location that Shakespeare called 'Aemonie' in *Macbeth*?
a **Inchcolm Island**

21 What runs all the way round Inverleith Park?
a **A bridle path**

22 What is buried in Corstorphine Old Parish Church that shouldn't really be there?
a **A sheepdog**

23 Where was the infamous 'Hole in the Ground'?
d **Castle Terrace**

24 What were the first Wester Hailes community centres nicknamed?
c **The Huts**

25 Where did Edinburgh's gypsy colony once reside?
c **Morningside**

26 Where was the original Traverse Theatre?
a **The West Bow**

27 According to legend, where does the well in the Royal Botanical Gardens lead?
b **Australia**

28 What is the road round Arthur's Seat known as?
c **The Radical Road**

29 Where do cyclists encounter a strange optical illusion on Arthur's Seat?
a **The Innocent Tunnel**

30 Where did Scotland's royals reside before Edinburgh?
c **Dunfermline**

31 Whose headquarters are at 121 George Street?
d **The Church of Scotland**

32 What was inspired by an ornamental pond in Queen Street Gardens?
a *Treasure Island*

33 Where did Sherlock Holmes investigate his first murder?
a **Lauriston Place**

34 What was first produced in Anchor Close in 1771?
c *The Encyclopaedia Britannica*

35 In Fishmarket Close lived Edinburgh's last what?
b **Hangman**

36 Which famous poet lived in Carruber's Close?
a **Alan Ramsay**

37 Sir Walter Scott and Robert Burns only met once. Where?
c **Sciennes House Place**

38 Which ethnic landmark is across the street from their meeting place?
b **A Jewish cemetery**

39 Where is the ruin of St Anthony's Chapel?
a **Arthur's Seat**

40 What was moved from Restalrig to Arthur's Seat?
a **St Margaret's Well**

41 What was Princes Street originally named, before George III lost his temper and demanded it be changed?
b **St Giles Street**

42 Which place is famous for its links with the ancient Knights Templar order and tales of the Holy Grail?

a Rosslyn Chapel, Roslin

43 Victims of the great plague in the 18th century were buried in which popular Edinburgh park?

c The Meadows

44 Where did Greyfriar's Bobby receive a bowl of food every day?

d Trail's Dining Room

45 Laurel and Hardy made their one-and-only appearance in Edinburgh at which cinema in 1939?

b Green's Playhouse

46 What is the name of Edinburgh's first new street since 1800?

d The Walk

47 Which Stockbridge street was once described by English poet Sir John Betjeman as the most attractive street in Edinburgh?

c Ann Street

48 The ashes of College Wynd were rebuilt as which street?

b Guthrie Street

49 Which place finally opened to foot traffic in 1786?

b South Bridge

50 Scotland's most famous duel, involving Court of Session judge Lord Shand in 1850, took place on a grassy slope below which famous Edinburgh landmark?

a Arthur's Seat

3 Buildings

1 What is the main tourist attraction at the Ocean Terminal Mall?
a **The former Royal Yacht *Britannia***

2 What is the nickname of the Leith high rise where the writer Irvine Welsh lived?
a **The Banana Block**

3 Where would you find The Tower restaurant?
c **The Museum of Scotland**

4 What is Jenners' claim to fame?
a **It's the world's oldest independent department store**

5 What is Sherlock Holmes's statue in Picardy Place frowning at?
b **A dog's footprint**

6 The address 1 Princes Street belongs to which premises?
b **Balmoral Hotel**

7 The cavernesque chambers of which pub inspired the idea for the 1995 hit movie *Shallow Grave*?
a **Bannermans**

8 What is the name of Hibernian football club's North Stand?
a **Famous Five Stand**

9 Which famous building on the south side sadly closed down in early 2004?
c **Odeon Cinema**

10 Why was Queen Victoria's statue moved from its original position outside Leith's Kirkgate centre?
c **To make way for a new monument**

11 In what type of building were the 2003 Europe MTV awards held?
c **A marquee tent**

12 Which popular music venue in Stockbridge's St Stephen Street was demolished before being rebuilt and turned into a restaurant?
c **Tiffany's**

13 What resided in the middle of the London Road/Elm Row roundabout before the current clock?
d **An abstract steel monument**

14 A full-scale model of which Edinburgh building is stored in New Zealand after the capital's Tattoo visited Wellington in the late 1990s?
a **Edinburgh Castle**

15 What was the name of Scotland's first (and shortlived) cannabis café?
b **The Purple Haze**

16 What was Edinburgh Castle's nickname in former times?
b **The Castle of Maidens**

17 What was the famous Boundary Bar renamed in 2003?
c **City Limits**

18 What is the Tron Church named after?
c **A weigh beam**

19 What was the name of Edinburgh's famous gay bar in the 1970s?
b **The Laughing Duck**

20 What was built out of 1,501,000 cartloads of earth from the foundations of Princes Street?
b **The Mound**

21 'The Wee Shop' based in Corstorphine is probably Scotland's smallest shop. How long is it?
b Four-and-a-half feet

22 Which phrase, constructed into gigantic letters, was strewn across a Dumbiedykes high-rise tenement?
a This Way Up

23 The Scotmid supermarket situated at the foot of Leith Walk was converted from what?
c Leith Central Station

24 Which of these *hasn't* been used as a venue for a Fringe production?
a A jail

25 The Forth Rail Bridge featured in scenes from which Alfred Hitchcock movie?
a *39 Steps*

26 What oddities adorned the walls and roof of the Green Tree Pub (formerly the Brown Cow)?
c Painted-on cracks

27 The castle esplanade was built in 1753 using rubble from what contemporary construction?
a The Royal Exchange

28 What was the Dean Gallery Building previously used as?
b An orphanage

29 The Festival Theatre in Nicholson Street was converted from what in the 1990s?
a A bingo hall

30 Where was Edinburgh's highest ever tenement?
b Parliament Square

31 What is reputed to be Edinburgh's oldest public house?
d The Beehive

32 What part of Edinburgh castle was built by French prisoners?
a The cobbled walkway

33 What building is famously described as 'Edinburgh's Disgrace'?
a The 12-columned acropolis on Calton Hill

34 The former GPO building on the east end of Princes Street is currently the capital's most high-profile what?
a Advertising site

35 What is unusual about St Andrews Catholic Church on Belford Road?
a It's made of wood

36 Which pub had its walls and roof covered in bizarre curiosities?
a The Canny Man

37 Who designed the National War Memorial Building?
d Sir Robert Lorrimer

38 What is the Scott Monument's nickname?
c The Gothic Rocket

39 Who founded the Advocate's Library?
a Sir George Mackenzie

40 Clermiston Tower was built to celebrate which famous Scot?
a Sir Walter Scott

41 Who built Holyrood Palace?

b Robert Mylne

42 Which building features Scotland's finest examples of pre-Reformation stained glass?
d The Magdalene Chapel

43 The design of Stewart's Melville College was originally intended for what building?
a The Houses of Parliament

44 What was odd about the service flats built in Orchard Brae between the World Wars?
a They didn't have kitchens

45 Where are the last timber galleries in Edinburgh?
c John Knox House

46 Edinburgh's first defensive wall was erected after what?
b The battle of Sark

47 What first opened in Ship Close in 1727?
a The Royal Bank of Scotland

48 What was discovered under 25 feet of rock and soil during the construction of the Union Canal in Kirkliston?
b The tusk of a mammoth

49 English prisoners had to leap a 12-foot gap between Borthwick Castle's towers if they wanted to be released But they had to jump with which handicap?
b With hands tied behind the back

50 The Frasers building on Princes Street was once known as Maules. What other name did it go by?
b Binns

4 History

1 In which year did Edinburgh become the capital of Scotland?

c **1633**

2 What was the name given to the plague of 1644?

a **The Black Death**

3 How many times in its past has Edinburgh actually been attacked?

a **17**

4 Trams will soon reappear on Edinburgh's streets. In which year did they stop running?

a **1957**

5 What was the service number of the last tram?

d **172**

6 Which of the following cities is Edinburgh not twinned with?

d **Oslo**

7 A mini tidal wave occurred in Leith as a result of offshore seismic activity. In which year did it happen?

d **1843**

8 One of Edinburgh's most spectacular riots occurred following the banning of which popular pageant?

a **Robin Hood**

9 What percentage of Edinburghers died during the plague?

b **20%**

10 In which year did the great fire of Edinburgh wipe out most of the High Street?

c **1824**

11 Which wall was built around the city centre to help defend Edinburgh in 1513?

b **Flodden Wall**

12 In 1924 Edinburgh's first what began operating?

c **Radio station**

13 What resulted in the cancellation of an historic theatrical occasion called by George V at the Empire Theatre in 1911?

a **A major fire**

14 What length of time did Bonnie Prince Charlie spend in Edinburgh during 1745?

c **Six weeks**

15 Burke and Hare were immigrants from which country?

c **Ireland**

16 What did the *Great Michael*, pride of Scotland's navy, end up as?

a **A French prison ship**

17 *Queen Margaret, Mary Queen of Scots, Robert The Bruce* and *Sir William Wallace* were the names of the last four what?

b **Ferry boats to Fife prior to the construction of the Forth Road Bridge**

18 What was the first vehicle pulled across the North Bridge when it opened?

b **A hearse**

19 What did George IV wear under his kilt at an Assembly Rooms ball?

b **Pink tights**

20 Who granted Edinburgh its first extant Royal Charter?
d Robert the Bruce

21 The many blocked-up windows in Edinburgh were an attempt to get round what?
a Window tax

22 In 1574 in Fountain Close, Thomas Bassendyne produced Scotland's first printed what?
a Bible

23 Under which act was Maggie Dixon tried and sentenced to hang?
a The Concealment of Pregnancy Act

24 Which British king was born in Edinburgh Castle?
a James VI

25 When did the city's bus lanes first appear?
a 1974

26 And on which street were they first visible?
a Earl Gray Street

27 What message was displayed on the floral clock in Princes Street Gardens to mark the end of WW2?
a Our Finest Hour

28 Why did Edinburgh University temporarily move to Linlithgow in 1645?
a The plague had broken out

29 What did the Romans call the Celtic tribe who first inhabited Edinburgh?
a The Votadini

30 What was plotted at the Sheep's Heid Inn in Duddingstone?
b The battle of Prestonpans

31 What were caddies?
a Street messengers

32 Which club, founded by William Smellie, had Robert Burns as a member?
a The Crochallan Fencibles

33 A disease referred to as 'The New Acquaintance' in 16th-century Edinburgh is known as what today?
b Influenza

34 The best-attended lecture in the history of Edinburgh's medical school came in 1829 The body of which person had been supplied to the school for dissection?
d William Burke

35 In which year did Princes Street's station, situated at the junction of Lothian Road and Rutland Street, close?
d 1965

36 Fourteen bombing raids were experienced in Edinburgh during WW2. How many died in the raids?
b 17

37 Following the 1707 Act of Union with England, what did some locals dub Edinburgh?
a A widowed metropolis

38 What did Lord Drumlanrig's son do while his father was witnessing the signing of the union?
a Eat a boy servant he'd roasted on a spit

39 The first Edinburgh history book was published in which year?
d **1792**

40 Where in Edinburgh did King Malcolm III build his hunting lodge?
c **Castle Rock**

41 Cloth sellers, beggars and fishwives' stalls on the High Street in the 15th century were known as what?
a **Luckenbooths**

42 Charles I's attempt to enforce his revision of the English Book of Common Prayer led to a riot in St Giles' Cathedral. What did cabbage seller Jenny Geddes throw at the minister to set it off?
a **A stool**

43 In 1328, the Treaty of Edinburgh ended which war that had taken place with England (in Scotland's favour)?
b **Wars of Independence**

44 George Bryce was the last man to be publicly hanged in 1864. How many people turned up to witness it?
c **20,000**

45 Name the processional ceremony that crowds stopped to watch during the opening of the old Scottish Parliament.
b **The Riding**

46 Edinburgh's first-ever traffic signal began operating on 21 March 1928, at which junction?
b **York Place/Broughton Street**

47 Where can you still find an old strip of tramline lying in the middle of the road?
c **Waterloo Place**

48 From what did citizens of Edinburgh and Leith come under attack on 2 April 1916?
c **Zeppelin bombers**

49 What was the former Waverley Market in Princes Street used for during WW1?
a **The manufacture of tank parts**

50 What happened to prisoners when the old prison in the High Street was demolished in 1817?
c **They moved to Calton Jail**

5 Sports and Leisure

1 What was first played at Edinburgh's Leith Links?
a Golf

2 The Leith Victoria AAC is Scotland's oldest what?
a Boxing club

3 Who are the sponsors on Hibs' jerseys?
b Carlsberg

4 What is the former name of Edinburgh's ice-hockey team?
b The Murrayfield Racers

5 What was Livingston FC's former name?
a Meadowbank Thistle

6 Where was the first ever International Rugby game played in 1871?
a Raeburn Place

7 Martin Bell is associated with which rather unexpected sport for an Edinburgher?
c Alpine skiing

8 Name the ex-Manchester United and Scotland footballer born and raised in Muirhouse?
b Gordon Strachan

9 When was the last time Hibs won the Scottish Cup?
b 1902

10 Who tried to amalgamate both Hearts and Hibs as one united team during the 1980s?
a Wallace Mercer

11 Name Hibernian's campaign to stop it from happening?
a Hands Off Hibs

12 Allan Wells won the 100 metres gold in the 1980 Moscow Olympics in how many seconds?
b 10.25

13 Gavin Hastings' record of 44 points scored in one test match lasted how long?
b One week

14 What was World Lightweight Champion Ken Buchanan's trademark?
b Tartan shorts

15 Channel swimmer Ned Barnie used to shock people at Portobello Pool by high diving into what?
b The shallow end

16 How many caps did Andy Irvine win in his ten-year career playing rugby for Scotland?
b 51

17 What was champion golfer Tommy Armour's nickname?
c The Silver Scot

18 Swimmer David Wilkie broke how many world, European and Commonwealth records in total?
c 30

19 What trophy did SPL team Livingston win in season 2003/4?
b League Cup

20 Chris Hoy won a gold medal in the 2002 Commonwealth Games for which sport?
b **Cycling**

21 In 2000 which Scottish National race did the swimmer Danielle Barclay win?
a **200 metres breaststroke**

22 Who are Hibs' Gordon Smith, Bobby Johnstone, Lawrie Reilly, Eddie Turnbull and Willie Ormand better known as?
b **The Famous Five**

23 What is the name of the Scottish American Football team who play their home games at Murrayfield Stadium?
d **The Scottish Claymores**

24 In 1938 the Hearts board proposed a move to a 'greenfield' site in which part of town?
d **Sighthill**

25 With which sport was former Hibs and Scotland goalkeeper Andy Goram also a Scottish internationalist?
b **Cricket**

26 For what was Hibernian's Easter Road ground pitch famous?
b **Its slope**

27 In which year were the first Commonwealth Games held in Edinburgh?
d **1970**

28 And the second?
d **1986**

29 At this event, Liz McColgan won gold in which race?
a **10,000 metres**

30 What did John Mutai win in June 2004?
a **The Edinburgh Marathon**

31 Stephane Adam scored in Hearts' Scottish Cup winning side of 1998. What nationality is he?
d **French**

32 Which team pipped Hearts to win the Scottish Premier League on the last game of the season in 1986?
c **Celtic**

33 Hearts' new footballing academy was set up in 2004. Where is it based?
b **Riccarton**

34 What is the name of the Edinburgh Speedway team?
a **The Monarchs**

35 What is the name of Edinburgh's Celtic League rugby team?
a **Gunners**

36 The women of ENC Onyx won the City of Edinburgh league for which sport?
c **Netball**

37 Which Hearts player scored a hat-trick against Rangers at Ibrox in 1996?
d **Allan Johnston**

38 What was the record attendance between Hibs and Hearts at Easter Road?
c **54,000**

39 Where did Hearts football club take their name from?

c **A dance hall called the Heart of Midlothian**

40 Where in Edinburgh is greyhound racing held?

a **Powderhall**

41 Which team did the Scotland rugby team play at its inauguration on 21 March 1925?

c **England**

42 What was the name of the vehicle Richard Noble drove when he broke the world land speed record in 1983?

b **Thrust 2**

43 What speed did his car reach?

c **638 mph**

44 David Wilkie claimed gold at the Montreal Olympics in 1976. What 200-metre race did he win?

b **Breaststroke**

45 What did Lachie Stewart say to the legendary Ron Clarke after beating him in the 10,000 metres at the 1970 Commonwealth Games?

a **Sorry**

46 Traditionally, archers competed in Edinburgh for which trophy?

a **The silver arrow**

47 Which sport, in 1701, was banned from the streets of Edinburgh because huge crowds brought traffic to a standstill?

b **Cockfighting**

48 Formed in 1838, the Edinburgh club for which sport is also the 'Mother Club' for this sport throughout the world?

c **Curling**

49 James II once banned golf at Leith Links because it interfered with which other sport?

a **Archery**

50 How did the great Edinburgh runner Eric Liddle die?

a **In a Japanese prison camp**

6 Customs

1 What language do the words 'Barry' and 'Raj' derive from?
b Romany

2 The Edinburgh slang word 'barry' is to say something is what?
a Good

3 Which day is reserved for late-night shopping in Edinburgh?
c Thursday

4 What are Hearts fans affectionately known as?
a The Jambos

5 Coburg Street was originally a tolerance zone for what?
a Prostitution

6 The Balmoral Hotel clock is deliberately fast so that you don't miss your train. But by how much?
d 2 minutes

7 Poet William Dunbar called Edinburgh 'a city of two contrasting faces: one rich, one poor'. These days people usually refer to Edinburgh as Pride and what?
a Poverty

8 What was carved above Willie Whitelaw's chair in St Giles' Thistle Chapel?
a A big bee

9 Which of Edinburgh's many drinking clubs met in Fleshmarket Close?
b The Marrowbone Club

10 Why is Edinburgh's main waterway called the Water of Leith, not the River of Leith?
b It's too small to be a river

11 At Saughton Prison, 8am was the set time for what?
c Executions

12 Which street is said to have been built in a single day?
b Lothian Road

13 What is Edinburgh's popular festive attraction in Princes Street called?
a Winter Wonderland

14 Edinburgh's nickname Auld Reekie was first coined by folk from where?
d Fife

15 Which meal of the day did the smoke bellowing above Edinburgh signal to them?
c Dinner

16 In the 18th century a byword for violence and unpredictability was The Edinburgh what?
a Mob

17 The tradition of emptying chamber pots out of multi-storey buildings was preceded by which cry?
a Gardey Loo

18 What would pedestrians hastily shout out from below?
a Haud yer haun

19 Marjory Kennedy-Fraser devoted much of her life to collecting and preserving what?

b **Gaelic songs**

20 What culinary landmark first opened in Chambers Street in the 1930s?

a **A Chinese restaurant**

21 What was a tulzie?

a **A large fight**

22 What could be found inside Anchor Close, and gave the close its name?

a **The Anchor Pub**

23 What character leads the famous Beltane Procession?

b **The Green Man**

24 The firm MacSweens is famous for making what?

d **Haggis**

25 What were gundies?

b **Sweets**

26 Edinburgh may well be named after which Northumbrian king?

a **Edwin of Deira**

27 What marked the limit of the Holyrood sanctuary for debtors?

d **The Girth Cross**

28 What were the debtors hiding in Holyrood sanctuary known as?

b **The Abbey Lairds**

29 What was on the Burgh of Leith coat of arms?

a **The Virgin and Child**

30 From where did the alleyways called 'closes' derive their name?

b **The word 'enclosure'**

31 You do not have to pay an entry fee to Edinburgh Castle if you only want to visit what?

d **The National War Memorial**

32 The one o'clock gun was established for what purpose?

d **To give an accurate time check to the ships in Leith Harbour**

33 What's interesting about the steps leading to Calton Road from the Black Bull pub?

a **Ewan MacGregor ran down them in *Trainspotting***

34 Every summer half-naked men and women parade through South Queensferry before plunging into the cold waters of the Forth. What's this tradition called?

a **The Loony Dook**

35 The opening lines of which writer's 'Address to Edinburgh' are 'Edina, Scotia's darling seat'?

c **Robert Burns**

36 By what name would older generations of Edinburgh and Leith remember the Northern General Hospital?

a **Leith Public Health Hospital**

37 The Newhaven Fishing Fleet was commonly referred to as what?

a **The Reaper of the Seas**

38 What, in local government circles, was known as the 'Greetin' Meetin'?

a **The last meeting before the elections**

39 Which famous Edinburgh firm was known by the popular name 'The Dummie'?

a Edinburgh and Dumfriesshire Dairy Co. Ltd

40 When were newspaper reporters first admitted to town council meetings?

c 1833

41 Why did Edinburghers name Alan Ramsay's house on Calton Hill 'Goose Pie'?

a Because of its shape

42 Can you describe a bell penny?

b Money put aside for a funeral

43 The lone piper is a traditional and popular feature at the Tattoo. In which year did the first-ever woman, Officer Cadet Elaine Marnoch, take on this role?

c 1977

44 What was referred to as a 'deid-chalk'?

a A meal eaten by officers after an execution

45 What was composed in a London Street house in 1874?

c The Icelandic national anthem

46 Local firm McVitie & Price were famed for their wedding cakes. For whom did they bake one in 1947?

a Princess Elizabeth and Prince Philip

47 What was known as The Presbytery?

a A club which met in Anchor Close

48 Traditionally, two city churches receive Christmas trees from the Queen. St Giles is one, but what is the other?

c Canongate

49 What marks the closing of the Edinburgh International Festival?

d A fireworks concert

50 The Latin term 'Nisi Dominus Frustra' is based on a passage from Psalm 127 Who uses it as their motto?

a City of Edinburgh

7 Weird Edinburgh

1 Diane's Pool Hall had the first L-shaped what in Britain?
a Pool table

2 What is the nickname given to the area dominated by lap-dancing strip bars?
a Pubic Triangle

3 Stolen traffic cones cost taxpayers in the capital thousands of pounds each year. How many are estimated missing per year?
c 2,000

4 Which swimming pool has nude-bathing sessions?
b Dalry

5 What marks the spot of the last public hanging in Edinburgh?
c An 'H' made of steel

6 What else does Broughton Street chip shop Piccante moonlight as?
a A night-club with DJs

7 A man was once charged by police for attempting to make love in public to what?
d A traffic cone

8 The Great Lafayette haunts which Edinburgh theatre?
d The Festival Theatre

9 And how did the Great Lafayette die?
c He died in a fire that started while he was on stage

10 The Mackenzie Poltergeist is said to haunt which Edinburgh site?
a Greyfriars Graveyard

11 To clean grass from the cobbles in Charlotte Square the unemployed used to be given what?
c Scissors

12 Which four-legged film star was photographed on the stairway of the Caledonian Hotel?
c Trigger

13 What was Edinburgh's fad for building railway lines in the early 18th century called?
b Railway Mania

14 Witchery tour guides are dressed as which notorious highwayman?
a Adam Lyal

15 According to legend the remnants of which notorious gang died in a shoot-out with police in Leith?
a The Ned Kelly Gang

16 Dr Richard Wiseman led the world's biggest scientific ghost hunt in the South Bridge Vaults in 2002. What was his conclusion?
b The 'ghosts' were imaginary

17 What were installed on the North Bridge, until repeated vandalism forced their removal?
a Samaritan telephone help lines

18 The Scotland Street tunnel was once used to investigate what?
b Material from space

19 There is a diary in the Royal Mile Police Museum made of what?
d Human skin

20 What is unusual about Edinburgh Zoo's only elephant?
d It's a statue

21 Which 17th-century book gave Mary King's Close its terrible reputation?
b *Satan's Invisible World*

22 Before it was stolen, in what odd place was one of the Forth Rail Bridge rivets displayed?
c The Central Library men's toilet

23 How did the Duchess of Gordon raise a Scottish regiment?
a By kissing each new recruit

24 What is unusual about the Marquis of Montrose's signature on the National Covenant?
b It appears to be written in blood

25 What did residents of Roseburn do when they heard the rumour that a WW2 German bomber had hit the brewery on Russell Road?
a They poured into the streets with empty jugs

26 By 1700 there were how many wigmakers in Edinburgh?
d 65

27 In 1842 Edinburgh had 200 what?
b Brothels

28 One of the most popular shows at the Fringe is called 'Puppetry of the' what?
d Penis

29 Why did goldsmith Alistir Tait alter the Church of Scotland's 'Moderator's Ring' in 2004?
a To fit the finger of the first woman Moderator

30 Council chiefs rapped the Burke & Hare lap-dancing bar in May 2004. Why?
a The exterior was painted silver and black

31 An image of Sir Walter Scott once advertised which product on an enamelled tin sign on Blair Street?
c Fountain pens

32 Who is said to haunt the White Hart Inn in the Grassmarket?
c Robert Burns

33 'X-Rayed Edinburgh' adorned badges given out to those who partook in the campaign against which disease in the 1950s?
d TB

34 Drag queen Lily Savage made his/her Scottish debut in which bar?
a Laughing Duck

35 Why, during medieval times, were steps to some Edinburgh houses deliberately made of varying height?
b So that unfamiliar 'visitors' might stumble and be heard

36 Which door can you find within the Beehive Inn on the Grassmarket?
a A condemned cell door from Calton Jail

37 On a famous trip to Edinburgh in 1822, George IV had to retire early from a dance at the Assembly Rooms. Why?

c **Someone dropped his pistol on his big toe**

38 There are 222,020 women in Edinburgh compared with how many men?

a **196,894**

39 The name Rose Street is also commonly used to describe which part of many European towns?

a **Red-light districts**

40 During 17th-century Edinburgh the burnt ashes of doves' dung were used to treat what?

d **Baldness**

41 What was the first animal to be bought by Edinburgh Zoo?

b **A gannet**

42 How much did it cost?

a **18p**

43 Of what did Western Union once say 'it's an interesting novelty without any commercial possibilities'?

a **Graham Bell's telephone**

44 'The Flowers of Scotland' was a popular nickname for the stench that emanated from the sewers between tenements. Where did the name originate?

c **In a fiddle tune**

45 In Broxburn, West Lothian, what became a bizarre tourist attraction at the turn of the 20th century?

a **A 100 foot-long icicle formed on the Union Canal**

46 What was produced to mark the phenomenon?

c **A postcard**

47 Why, for a time in the 1700s, did magistrates order the slaughter of all dogs?

a **A butcher's dog went mad**

48 An ancient privilege of the doorkeepers at the Court of Session is to demand a 5-shilling penalty from any noisy individual who wears what?

a **Spurs**

49 On average, how many hours of bright sunshine does Edinburgh receive a year?

a **1351**

50 How much will it cost you to have City of Edinburgh Council provide you with a weekday burial and lair?

c **£1,233**

8 The Arts

1 Author Irvine Welsh is most famous for which book?

a Trainspotting

2 There are several statues of which animals at the top of Leith Walk

a Pigeons

3 Who used to perform weekly at Clowns Bar?

c The Proclaimers

4 What inspired Dickens's *Christmas Carol*?

c The headstone of Ebenezer Scroggie

5 Peter Cook, Dudley Moore, Alan Bennett and Jonathan Millar made up which Festival comedy team?

b Beyond the Fringe

6 Where is the Edinburgh Book Festival traditionally held?

a Charlotte Square

7 Who is the Morningside cat made famous in a series of children's books?

a Maisie

8 Muriel Spark's Miss Jean Brodie was modelled on Christina Kay. Who was she?

d Her teacher

9 What famous author drinks in the Oxford Bar?

a Ian Rankin

10 What was the name of the female lead singer of the band The Rezillos?

c Faye Fife

11 What was the name of Edinburgh's first performance poetry club?

b The Big Word

12 In the 19th century John Kay was famous in Edinburgh for producing what?

a Caricatures

13 For which subject was the sculptor Sir John Steell the most famous in Britain?

d Horses

14 What was the most famous work of the poet Alan Ramsay?

c 'The Gentle Shepherd'

15 What was the 19th-century writer Susan Ferrier known as?

b Scotland's Jane Austen

16 Where was the Scottish Book Trust headquarters before moving to Trunk's Close?

a Above Fountainbridge Library

17 Which one of these was *not* discovered at the Festival Fringe?

b Ben Elton

18 Which of these works did author John Gay write?

a The Beggar's Opera

19 What is Jack Vettriano's best-known painting?

b *The Singing Butler*

20 T.S. Eliot's famous poems inspired the musical *Cats*, what were they based on?

d Stray cats in Greyfriars

21 Which famous Scottish violinist was painted by Sir Henry Raeburn?
a **Niel Gow**

22 Who carved the large rounded sculptures in the gardens of the Gallery of Modern Art?
a **Henry Moore**

23 What was architect Sir Basil Spence's most famous and controversial design?
c **Coventry Cathedral**

24 The artist Phoebe Traquair was Edinburgh's most acclaimed exponent of which style?
a **Art Deco**

25 In the statue in the City Chambers Courtyard what is the name of the horse that Alexander is wrestling?
b **Bucepheles**

26 What was Rab in John Brown's book *Rab and His Friends*?
c **A mastiff**

27 What was the painter Alexander Nasmyth known as?
b **Father of the Scottish Landscape**

28 Who was the first director of the Edinburgh Festival?
a **Rudolph Bing**

29 Which now-famous poet was born and died in poverty in the Cowgate?
a **William McGonagall**

30 Who *hasn't* appeared at Murrayfield Stadium?
d **Cliff Richard**

31 What first hit Edinburgh's streets on 25 June 1993?
a **The first Scottish *Big Issue***

32 Which folk singer was also an art teacher at St Serfs?
b **Donnie Munroe**

33 Edinburgh and Kirriemuir have Britain's only two working examples of what?
b **Camera Obscuras**

34 Who designed the giant 'foot' outside St Mary's Cathedral?
a **Eduardo Paolozzi**

35 The musician Matthew Hardie was known as what?
b **The Scottish Stradivari**

36 Who persuaded Robert Louis Stevenson to make Dr Jekyll and Mr Hyde the same person?
a **His wife**

37 Sir Harry Lauder was the first British artist to do what?
a **Sell a million records**

38 Which famous phrase was invented by Robert Louis Stevenson?
b **The Land of Nod**

39 Which well-known author was born in Castle Street in 1859?
a **Kenneth Grahame**

40 Who wrote the original book *Greyfriars Bobby*?
a **Eleanor Atkinson**

41 Which cartoon superhero battled a villain on Edinburgh Castle's ramparts in a famous episode of his comic book?

c Batman

42 Where would you find sculptures of a group of chickens?

b Kinnaird Park

43 Guarding Edinburgh Zoo's old gatehouse are statues of what?

d Golden Eagles

44 Who paid for the poet Robert Fergusson's headstone?

b Robert Burns

45 What was Edinburgh's famous punk band called?

a The Exploited

46 Anthony Daniels opened the Star Wars exhibition at the Market Street Art Exhibition Centre in 2001. Which character did he play in the saga?

c C3PO

47 Which Edinburgh publisher first printed Irvine Welsh's *Trainspotting*?

b Rebel Inc.

48 At the 2003 MTV Europe Awards held in Leith, which act was introduced flying over Edinburgh in a computer-generated spaceship?

c The Darkness

49 Founded by Mike Hart, the jazz festival is the longest-running in the country. In which year was it founded?

c 1978

50 DCC Bob Skinner has investigated many crimes in Edinburgh. But who is his creator?

a Quintin Jardine

9 Leading and Lagging

1 Edinburgh's Hogmanay celebrations were cancelled on New Year's Eve 2003. What was the official reason for postponing the event?
a Bad weather

2 What name was given to the new cloned sheep at the Roslin Institute near the city?
c Dolly

3 There was an outcry when the Scottish Parliament spent an additional £663,000 so that MSPs could each have what?
c A widescreen TV

4 At a cost of £19,000 to the tax payer Parliament bosses have also fitted MSPs' offices with which item?
c Fridge

5 In the 1970s, trains took 43 minutes to go from Glasgow Central to Waverley Station. How long is the average journey now?
c 50 minutes

6 Which of these did *not* go to Edinburgh University Medical School?
b Joseph Lister

7 Who wrote what is now regarded as the first published theory of evolution?
c James Burnett

8 James Young Simpson was a pioneer of which medical marvel?
b Chloroform

9 Which of these was *not* on display at Ingliston's Classic Car Museum?
b Basil Fawlty's Mini

10 Due to public outcry several attempts in the 1990s to build a memorial to whom were abandoned?
d The Bodysnatchers

11 How much did Leith's new mini-hospital, The Leith Community Treatment Centre, cost to build?
c £8 million

12 What is the name given to Edinburgh's unique bus lanes?
b Greenways

13 The Forth Railway Bridge is known as the what 'Wonder of the World'?
b Eighth

14 In 1862, how long did it take to travel from London to Edinburgh aboard *The Flying Scotsman* steam train?
a 10-and-a-half hours

15 The 18th century is known in Edinburgh as the 'Age of ' what?
b Improvement

16 Which new Edinburgh festival recently attracted 1,500 visitors from as far away as Germany and America?
a The Dark City Goth Festival

17 The City of Edinburgh Car-Free Festival cost the taxpayer £100,000. What did city leader Donald Anderson call it?
d A gimmick

18 Which Edinburgh hotel won the 2004 Scottish Hotel Restaurant of the Year award?
c Balmoral Hotel

19 Edinburgh could soon be hosting the qualifying events and training camps for which prestigious event?

b 2012 Olympic Games

20 Edinburgh Castle was the nation's top paid-for tourist attraction in 2004. What came second?

b Edinburgh Zoo

21 How will new buses running between Edinburgh Castle and Holyrood Palace be powered?

d Electricity

22 What opened in 1507 at the foot of Blackfriars Wynd, and was the very first in Scotland?

b Printing press

23 The first anti-tobacco tract – Counterblast Against Tobacco – was written by whom?

d James VI

24 Edinburgh is bidding to become a UNESCO-designated World City of what?

a Literature

25 Today, the North Bridge can carry a vehicle weighing up to how many tonnes?

b 40

26 It was estimated that the Forth Road Bridge would cost 3 million pounds. How much was the eventual bill?

c 19 million

27 How wide is the Forth Road Bridge?

a 58 feet

28 What excuse was given for taking nine years to complete the building of the George IV Bridge?

a Lack of funds

29 The Midlothian County Council once demolished an entire street to make way for its offices. Which street was it?

d Melbourne Street

30 What took 3 years and a quarter of a million pounds to complete?

a Edinburgh–Glasgow railway line

31 George Chalmers financed the Chalmers Hospital with £30,000 of his own money. What was his occupation?

c Plumber

32 The Playfair Project opened in August 2004, providing a link between which two buildings?

d The National Gallery and the Royal Scottish Academy

33 According to the Royal National Institute of the Blind, how many Edinburgh firms said it would be difficult or impossible to employ someone partially sighted or blind?

d 9 out of 10

34 Those who didn't pay their 'poor rates' in 1894 wouldn't have been able to what?

b Vote

35 With each of its 48 rooms fitted with PC, DVD and Hi-Fi, the Bonham Hotel is staking a claim to the title of the 'World's Most' what 'Guest House'?

b Wired

36 Charles Higham described Edinburgh as a 'dignified spinster with' what?
d **Syphilis**

37 Edinburgh has a high ratio of accountants. How many are there registered at present?
b **1322**

38 The troubled Scottish Parliament superseded its original estimated cost of £30 million. What was the final estimated cost?
b **£431 million**

39 Leading architect Andrew Doolan won a Royal Institute of British Architects award for Dick House. Where in town can it be found?
c **The Grange**

40 What will cost £1 billion and have towers constructed from reinforced concrete?
a **A new transport bridge to be built to the west of the Forth Road Bridge**

41 The council's controversial road tolls are estimated to cost £429 million. But how much will it cost to cross its cordons into the city?
b **£2**

42 Which club was forced to make way for the City of Edinburgh Council's new home in New Street?
c **The Bongo Club**

43 Sir Patrick Geddes created plans for over 20 cities in India as well as for Edinburgh. Where will a new glass sculpture of him be situated?
a **Outside the new council headquarters on East Market Street**

44 A new civic square in the heart of Munich is to be named after Edinburgh to mark 50 years of friendship between the two cities. What will it be called?
d **The Edinburghplatz**

45 Days after announcing the closure of Fountainbridge Brewery, Scottish and Newcastle's yearly profit was revealed as how much?
b **£471 million**

46 Chloroform looked set to remain a local medical fad until what happened?
a **Queen Victoria started using it**

47 How many murders was the mass killer William Burke finally convicted of?
a **One**

48 James Rutherford was the inventor of what?
c **The gas lamp**

49 In 1842 Thomas Sturrock and Charles Drummond invented what?
a **The Christmas card**

50 James Hutton is known as the father of what?
b **Geology**

10 Miscellaneous

1 Complete the phrase Glaswegians often use to describe Edinburghers: 'All fur coat and nae' what?
d Knickers

2 What is the name of the popular Fringe theatre venue that was once a mental institution?
b Bedlam

3 Edinburgh Zoo is renowned for which animals?
a Penguins

4 What's unique about the bar Fingers in Frederick Street?
a It's Edinburgh's only official piano bar

5 Edinburgh's only Russian bar is called Da Da Da. What does it mean in English?
b Yes Yes Yes

6 Harry Potter author J.K. Rowling used to write about the boy wizard from which coffee house?
a The Elephant House

7 The *Scotsman* newspaper once published a review of a rock show that never took place. Which artist was in question?
d Meat Loaf

8 How many monarchs have landed at Leith?
b Three

9 People flock to Edinburgh to study at its universities. Approximately how many students are there?
a 33,500

10 Which city did Robert Louis Stevenson say Edinburgh ought to be like?
c Paris

11 Environmental visitor centre Dynamic Earth's slogan maintains you can live how many 'million years in one day'?
d 2,400

12 The Water of Leith is how many miles long?
c 28

13 Leith pipped Edinburgh to open which shop first?
c Woolworths

14 Where did Sir Walter Scott find Edinburgh's missing crown jewels?
b In a chest in Edinburgh Castle

15 What is different about the 'E' and 'U' in the City of Edinburgh Council's logo?
b The colour

16 According to lore, what did the devil predict from the steps of the Mercat Cross?
b The battle of Flodden

17 What was Scotland's largest street brawl called?
a The Cleansing of the Causeway

18 What in Edinburgh Castle is 110 feet deep?
a The Castle well

19 What was used to secure a fresh body so that it couldn't be stolen?
a Mortice locks

20 What were the Pickwick, the Owl and the Waverly?

b Pens

21 Who does the statue outside the Sheraton Hotel reputedly represent?

d Winnie Mandela

22 What is confusing about the statue of Sir Walter Scott inside the Scott Monument on Princes Street?

a It's not the famous writer

23 One is lying down outside Leith Theatre while another pushes a barrel. They are statues of what?

b Sailors

24 While staying at the Balmoral Hotel, Velvet Underground singer, Lou Reed, sent a drink back nine times because they couldn't make it 'taste right.' What type of drink was it?

b Coffee

25 Derek Dick is one of Edinburgh's most famous rock singers. By what name is he better known?

b Fish

26 Brightly patterned squares on certain Lothian Buses are based on a Versace dress worn by which Hollywood actress?

b Liz Hurley

27 What did Green MSP Robin Harper have to dash off and purchase before being sworn into the Scottish Parliament in 1999?

b A tie

28 In Irvine Walsh's **Porno**, the sequel to **Trainspotting**, from which bar does Francis Begbie finally spot his double-crossing pal, Mark Renton?

d The Central Bar

29 Which film set in Edinburgh marked the debut production of Elton John's Rocket Pictures?

c *Women Talking Dirty*

30 How long will public tours at the new Scottish Parliament building last?

b 45 minutes

31 What did **Wired** magazine call The Malmaison Hotel?

c Rock 'n' roll

32 Corstorphine Hill has a radio mast, a ruined tower, and a boundary with the wild plains of Africa (at the Zoo). What else does it have that few people know about?

a A vast redundant nuclear shelter

33 Edinburgh's biggest gay nightclub, CC Blooms, is named after Bette Midler's character in which film?

c *Beaches*

34 The Dominion cinema in Morningside is Edinburgh's oldest independent cinema What film was showing when it opened its doors for the first time on 31 January 1938?

c *Wee Willy Winky*

35 Kurt Cobain once played an acoustic charity gig in Edinburgh. Where was it held?

d Southsider Bar

36 What is the exact length of the Royal Mile?

d **1 mile, 100 yards**

37 What are the official colours of Lothian Regional Transport's buses?

a **Douche Maroon and White**

38 Which theatre staged its first West End musical, selling out a 14-week run in 1989?

d **Playhouse**

39 How many trains are said to pass over the Forth Rail Bridge every 24 hours?

d **200**

40 What is the name of the Robert Louis Stevenson poem inscribed on a plaque outside his Heriot Row home?

b **The Lamplighter**

41 The Revolution night-club on Lothian Road was once home to which cinema?

b **Caley Cinema**

42 Jenners co-founder Charles Jenners once described Edinburgh women as 'the best' what 'in the Kingdom'?

a **Dressed**

43 The clock above Frasers department store used to play music. One tune was Caller Herrin. What was the other?

c **Scotland the Brave**

44 What is the name of the Belgian mirrored tent that has become a favourite at the Edinburgh International Book Festival?

d **The Speigeltent**

45 Pop star Prince performed in Edinburgh in the early 1990s. Where was the gig held?

d **Meadowbank Stadium**

46 The Rosslyn Chapel near Edinburgh was built by William Sinclair, a grand master of the Knights Templar. What was suggested as his reasons for building it?

b **To house the Holy Grail**

47 SSP Drugs Spokesman Kevin Williamson disrupted the Scottish Parliament in 2003 with a one-man protest in the public gallery. Who was he mimicking?

c **President George W. Bush**

48 What do Dalry Road, King's Stables Road, Morrison Street, Castle Terrace, Dewar Place Lane, Lothian Road, Torphichen Street, Torphichen Place, and Canning Street all have in common?

a **They're all streets lying above the Haymarket railway tunnel**

49 What is Edinburgh's Fools & Heroes?

a **A fantasy live role-playing society**

50 Street entertainer 'Silver' has been busking on Princes Street for well over 15 years. What does his act incorporate?

b **Robotics**

HOW DID YOU DO?

Score	Comment
401–500	Ya dancer! You're an Edinburgher of the capital variety. Are you sure you're not Sir Walter Scott in disguise?
301–400	Barry! You clearly ken more about Edinburgh than the Lord Provost. Here, have the freedom of the city, ya radge.
201–300	You're probably a Fifer, but hey, nobody's perfect. With a bit more salt 'n' sauce on your chips you'll be an Edinburgher before you know it.
101–200	Get back across the M8, weegie. You might know the difference between Holyrood and Hollywood, but you're fooling nobody.
0–100	See that big thing up there? Looks a bit like a castle? You've got three guesses and the first two don't count.